Jim Putman and Bobby Harrington not only will remind you of the importance of the Great Commission but also will spur you on to make lasting change in your ministry. If you want to realign the values of your church so that discipleship is at the core, read this book.

—Greg Surratt, Lead Pastor,
Seacoast Church; author, *Ir-Rev-Rend*

This book is good stuff. Bobby and Jim have long believed that the effectiveness of the church's mission depends largely on its capacity to make disciples. In *DiscipleShift* they say why they think that this is the case as well as show us how to make the shift. I recommend this book to everyone seeking to make discipleship a big deal in the local church.

—Alan Hirsch, founder,
Forge Mission Training Network

DiscipleShift is an incredible and practical resource for everyone serious about helping people follow Jesus. Jim and Bobby have generously shared what they've learned from their combined total of more than fifty years of ministry both in planting churches and leading thriving ones. I'm thrilled to see them share their experience in the area of discipleship. Leaders everywhere will do well to heed their advice.

—Jud Wilhite, Senior Pastor,
Central Christian Church

DiscipleShift brilliantly lays out the five shifts every church must make to develop more and better disciples of Jesus. Jim Putman has led Real Life Church to make these shifts and with great authenticity tell us how. If you are interested in disciple-making, this book is for you.

—Dave Ferguson, Lead Pastor,
Community Christian Church

Without discarding the church as it is, this book casts a beautiful vision for the church as it can be. Every church leader can grab hold of this vision and take their church through a "disciple shift."

—Dave Stone, Pastor, Southeast Christian

It seems everyone in church leadership is talking about making disciples. Jim Putnam and Bobby Harrington are actually doing it. They have teamed up with the foremost champion of discipleship, Robert E. Coleman, who has dedicated his life to making disciplemakers. The authors provide the church with a gift of a biblically robust and well-researched explanation of making disciples, coupled with practical implications that can be applied in any church passionate about making disciple-makers.

—Scott Thomas, Pastor of Ministry Development, The Journey; author, *Gospel Coach*

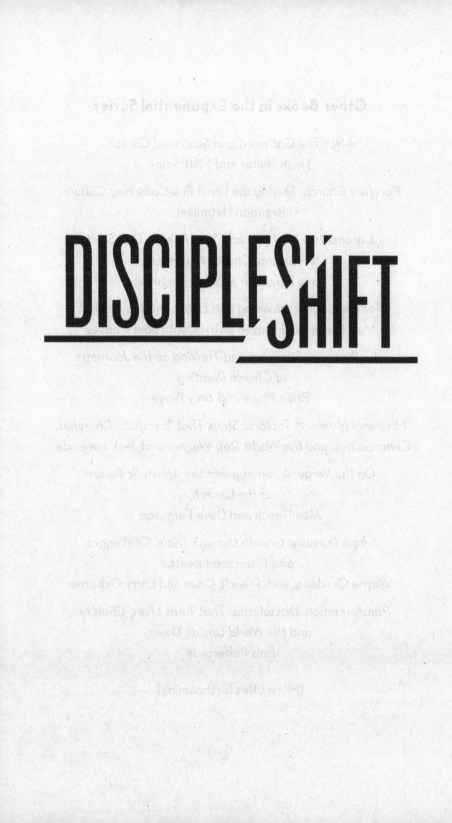

DISCIPLESHIFT

Other Books in the Exponential Series

(More titles forthcoming)

EXPONENTIAL
series

DISCIPLESHIFT

Five Steps That Help Your Church
to Make Disciples Who <u>Make</u> Disciples

JIM PUTMAN & BOBBY HARRINGTON
WITH ROBERT E. COLEMAN

ZONDERVAN°

ZONDERVAN.com/
AUTHORTRACKER
follow your favorite authors

We want to hear from you. Please send your comments about this book to us in care of zreview@zondervan.com. Thank you.

ZONDERVAN

DiscipleShift
Copyright © 2013 by Jim Putman and Bob Harrington

This title is also available as a Zondervan ebook. Visit www.zondervan.com/ebooks.

Requests for information should be addressed to:

Zondervan, *Grand Rapids, Michigan 49530*

Library of Congress Cataloging-in-Publication Data

Putnam, Jim, 1966.
    DiscipleShift : five steps that help your church to make disciples who make disciples / Jim Putman and Bobby Harrington with Robert Coleman.
    pages cm.
    Includes bibliographical references (pages 232-236).
    ISBN 978-0-310-49262-7 (softcover)
    1. Discipling (Christianity) I. Harrington, Bobby, 1958- II. Coleman, Robert Emerson, 1928 III. Title. IV. Title: Disciple shift.
BV4520.P875 2013
253—dc23   2012043590

Cover design: Ron Huizinga
Cover photography: Getty Images / Sorin Brinzei
Interior design: David Conn

Printed in the United States of America

13 14 15 16 17 18 19 20 /DCI/ 20 19 18 17 16 15 14 13 12 11 10 9 8 7 6 5 4 3 2 1

To my parents, Bill and Bobbie, and my wife and children

—Jim

To my good friend David Sanders, and my wife and children

—Bobby

CONTENTS

FOREWORD

Something is missing in the life of the church. Today's institution has a polite form of religion, but it seems to lack power, the power to radically change the wayward course of society. This is not to say that nothing worthwhile is happening. In fact, all kinds of things are going on, and if success is measured by big meetings, big buildings, and big budgets, then the church appears to be doing quite well.

But the real question has to be asked: is all this business actually fulfilling the mandate of Christ to make disciples and teaching them, in turn, to do the same? That's the mission of the church. Yes, we want churches to grow, but it is becoming painfully evident that getting more people on the rolls has not resulted in a corresponding increase in transformed lives. Where do you find the contagious sacrifice and all-out commitment to the Great Commission? In our obsession with bigger numbers of converts, far too little attention has been given to the nurture of believers in how to live their faith. This neglect has created a crisis in the contemporary church. How we deal with it, I believe, represents the most important issue we face today.

That's why the concern of this book is urgent. The book comes to grips with the problem of respectable superficiality in the house of God, and what can be done about it. The authors go back to the Bible and recognize in the way Jesus made disciples an example all of us can follow. We don't need crowds to reach the world. True, our Lord did on occasion speak to multitudes, but most of his time was spent with a few learners. Being with him day after day was the essence of their training. Ministry was seen not as a specialized clerical calling but as an everyday lifestyle of obedience to Christ.

Replicating this pattern of living becomes the goal of the priesthood of all believers.

Building on this, authors Jim Putman and Bobby Harrington set forth a plan by which intentional discipleship, developed through personal and group relationships, becomes the center of church life. Adjustments can be made to accommodate different situations and cultures, of course, but the biblical principles offer guidelines for implementation in any context. When this view of ministry is entirely new to a congregation that wants to start, helpful directions are suggested in transitioning to the model.

Giving the book a ring of authenticity is the personal experience of the authors. These are pastors who write out of what they have practiced. The validity of their teaching can be seen in their own growing churches, as well as the network of fellowships inspired by their example.

Here is an answer to the aimlessness and lack of spiritual depth in so much of the church growth we see today. It is down to earth. It isn't complicated. Even better, it presents a way to change the world, one person at a time. Not everyone will agree with all that they read, but you cannot read it without being challenged. And for those who dare to take its message to heart, the book may open a door to an exciting new concept of ministry.

—Dr. Robert E. Coleman

INTRODUCTION

Some of you are under real pressure.

You need to make things happen in your church. (And preferably by next Sunday!) You're seeing a decline in attendance, interest, passion, spiritual maturity, outreach, giving, evangelism, or effectiveness, and you need—actually, you *long*—to reverse those trends. You pray your church will be successful in its purpose. You want it to be as effective as possible. You're looking for a coach to provide a clear and uncomplicated way forward to biblical success. It's our prayer that this book will do that, and do so in a big way.

But right from the start, I (Jim) invite you to slow down and resist the urge to jump straight to a solution. This may seem counterintuitive, particularly for hard-driving leaders. But the reason for slowing down is this: in the same manner that it takes time for any church to develop its problems, it also takes time to sort out solutions and apply them to your church's specific context and situation. Church leaders are often tempted to read a book or attend a conference and then immediately attempt to change their church to the next great thing, whatever that may be. They seek one-size-fits-all, step-by-step remedies, plans that can be slapped on churches quickly. But that's not what this book is about.

I've seen leaders succumb to this temptation. Each month about a hundred church leaders from across the country attend our church's training and development program, the two-day event where we teach discipleship processes experientially and in depth. Formerly we held these programs at the beginning of the week, on Mondays and Tuesdays. Leaders could come into Post Falls, Idaho, where our church is located, and first attend a weekend service at our church, then attend the training program. But we don't do it that way anymore. Now we hold training sessions at the end of the week, on Thursdays and Fridays. There's strategy at work here. Now we hold the training first. Leaders can attend one of our church services afterward, if they wish.

The problem was that leaders used to attend one of our services, take a cursory look around, and then immediately jump to conclusions. They would tell me they had found our "secret." I'd always ask them what that was. They would say something like, "Ah, you've got great music. That's what we need." They might also say, "Your church is friendly and it makes people want to come back, so we need to do that as well."

But they missed it. Music isn't the issue (though I want the best music we can get in our church). Chances are good that the issue plaguing their church is much more important than what kind of music they use. It is true that if we want to give people a taste of relationship on the weekend, we want to be friendly, but that isn't the solution by itself either. A church won't go to the core to fix the problem if all it sees are the peripheral things.

It's like a professional baseball pitcher who develops a shoulder problem. He wants to keep playing, so he gets a trainer to shoot his shoulder full of cortisone, a drug that reduces inflammation and swelling at the site of an injury. The shoulder is numbed so the athlete can keep playing, but the athlete hasn't addressed the injury. He goes out on the field and is able to keep playing for a while, but soon his injury gets worse and catches up with him—and then he's out of the game for a long time, if not for good.

That's what happens when a leader simply imposes a new quick fix, peripheral solution on top of a core foundational mistake the church is already making. The symptoms are addressed, but the cause isn't. This book goes to the core, and it takes time to do that.

Another reason not to jump immediately to a solution, even if you rightly diagnose the problem, is that churches tend to move slowly through change. Think icebergs or large ships. Wise leaders need to go slowly toward any new cultural change or methodology. No matter what your church's age, if it's been meeting for more than a few months, then you will already have established ways of doing things, and the people are there because they like these practices. Every church has a preexisting DNA. Respect the people in your church, who they are, what your church's emphasis and methodologies are. The existing emphasis and methodology might be ineffectual, but your church has reasons for doing what it does and it will take time to lead through change.

Slow down, and steer your ship slowly and wisely. Learn what the core solution is to your church's problems, and then work with your team and with the specifics of your church's situation to implement change in effective and lasting ways.

There are always two issues at stake: choosing the right destination and choosing the right leadership style and way to get your people to the right destination. If you are a good leader who leads everyone to the wrong place, then you have failed. If you have the right destination but lead the wrong way, then you have also failed, because no one will follow you to the right place. I have seen both problems manifested more than once, so my advice is to take your time to do both right.

Are you with me?

It's no easy matter to shift how a local church operates so that it can become more effective. I'd be the first to admit that our church does not have all the answers, and we have made many mistakes along the way. We have struggled to discern the difference between a biblical principle that works everywhere and in every generation because it is God's design, and a principle that works only in our context.

Every leader will need to do the same. You will need to carefully discover how the biblical mandate works in your situation, and then have the wisdom to lead as a good shepherd leads to the right place. Even though we've made our share of mistakes, what we have experienced in the past years — and what we experience now — is so exciting, so fulfilling, so opposite of what so many experience in churches across the country, that we can't help but share the story of what God is doing. My goal in the pages to come is to highlight biblical principles pertaining to the mission of the church and note how these principles work in any context or culture.

If you are a church planter, let me also caution you. The great thing about starting a new church is that you can start everything fresh and new. The DNA of the new church will be the one that you and your team are creating—and everyone who has ever planted a church knows the initial thrill of planning with a blank slate. You say to yourself with great anticipation, "We get to create the church that has been birthed in our hearts by God."

But, as many church planters later realize, it is easy to jump in and attempt to create something new and different, only to find that you inadvertently end up creating something very similar to what you have known. You did not realize that many of your assumptions and practices were grounded in ways of doing church that hurt what you felt God leading you to create. The adage "measure twice, cut once" is helpful at this point. If we want to create a church truly committed to discipleship, every assumption about church needs to be filtered and reevaluated through the lens of the Scriptures and especially Jesus' methods for doing discipleship and church.

I've asked two leaders and key thinkers in the discipleship movement to help me write this book. We're going to keep the book in the "I" voice mostly, just so you know who's talking (Jim), but I want to give you a brief introduction to my coauthors and let you know what their role is in this book's writing.

Dr. Bobby Harrington is the founding and lead pastor of Harpeth Community Church just outside of Nashville, Tennessee. His church was launched in 1998 and at first used the attractional model, but it has since made the transition to the relational-discipleship model, the one this book espouses. Bobby knows firsthand what it means to shift a church's main focus to discipleship. In the last ten years, he has also trained and coached hundreds of church planters. He also has four degrees in theology, including a doctor of ministry degree from Southern Baptist Seminary, so his focus in this book will be on research and clarification, as well as helping to undergird this book's message with biblical truth.

Dr. Robert Coleman is a legend in the evangelical community. At age eighty-four, he's seen many examples of how a church can shift its focus to discipleship and go from floundering to thriving.

In 1963, Dr. Coleman wrote a book called *The Master Plan of Evangelism*, which has since sold multiple millions of copies all over the world. It was the first book I read on the topic of discipleship, and it has influenced my focus ever since. Dr. Coleman is a mentor of mine and will be adding sidebars throughout this book to help shed time-tested light on the subject.

In the following chapters, we'll examine what it means to shift our churches to focus on biblical discipleship in relational environments. My encouragement to all of us is to stay pliable, humble, and teachable. Let's engage and participate in the concepts presented in this book. And let's work together from the core out. If we focus on the philosophy first, on why change is needed, then we can know why things are done and adapt our thinking to our church's particular situation. First comes philosophy. Second comes practical adaptation. (Know the "why" before you figure out the "how.") You'll notice that each main shift is presented in two chapters. The first chapter of each shift focuses more on the philosophy behind the shift, and the second chapter focuses more on the methodology. (With the first shift, we've included two chapters on methodology because there is so much material there.)

Be encouraged that we are not alone in this. God always shows up and does his part perfectly. As you examine the teachings in this book and relate them to your church's situation, God will help you discern biblical principles versus personal preferences. He rewards people who seek him, and we need God's strength to get us out of our comfort zones and proceed.

Whatever your role in your church, whatever your level of learning, no matter if you've been a Christian for thirty years or thirty weeks, God is going to do something remarkable in and through you and through the local church you're an integral part of.

Okay, let's begin.

KEY POINTS

- Resist the urge to jump straight to a solution. Too many leaders are tempted to read a book or attend a conference and then immediately change their church to the next great thing, whatever that may be. That's not what this book is about.
- It's no easy matter to shift how a local church operates so that it can become more effective. Slow down, and steer your ship slowly and prudently. Learn what the core solution is to your church's problems, and then work with your team and with the specifics of your church's situation to implement change in effective and lasting ways.
- We're with you in this! The body of Christ is a team, and even as we write this book, we're praying for you and your church's success.

Chapter 1

THE ENGINE THAT DRIVES IT ALL

What is the God-given purpose of the local church?

Bobby Harrington gave a lot of his extra time for about a decade to train church planters and create church planting networks. He did it joyfully. But one day, flying out of Nashville for a network meeting in another city, a vague thought became a clear realization: he was uneasy with the churches being planted. Would the result of all these church planting efforts really last? Would the churches planted truly please God, long term?

The church planters were godly, wonderful people. The theology was good. Their level of commitment was inspiring. But he wondered if the approach to church planting that he and his peers (including various church planting organizations) were advocating was often leading to a shallow, cultural Christianity. Before giving himself to church planting, he had already concluded the same thing about many established churches. Too often they had problems with legalism or traditionalism or they lacked authenticity or something else that missed Jesus' heart for a lost and hurting world. But that day, he finally admitted to himself that he was witnessing much of the same cultural Christianity in the church planting world. Something at a fundamental level needed reevaluation.

It was around this time that we (Jim and Bobby) became good friends. We had the same fundamental belief. Maybe you agree with us? When it comes to the local church in North America today, something is not working.

The big question driving this book is the question of effectiveness. For a moment, resist the urge to defend yourself or your church. Don't defend your experience in ministry, your seminary degrees, or your genuine heart for seeing people come to know Christ. Don't defend any of the activities taking place at your church. And don't defend the size of your congregation, the amount of giving, your service to the poor, or the number of new converts. Simply ask yourself, Is the church producing results? Is it doing its job in the best way possible? And please resist the urge to quickly answer yes.[1]

It's true that throughout North America today, though numbers are declining, there are still many people coming to church, and some are busy with ministry-related activities. There are ministries to the poor. Buildings are being built. Programs are running at full tilt. Money is being given.

But attendance, busyness, construction, finances, and programs are not real indications of success. The core question of effectiveness — the question that ultimately matters — is whether the people who are getting saved are being conformed to the likeness of Christ. Are we making mature disciples of Jesus who are not only able to withstand the culture but are also making disciples of Jesus themselves?

Let's look at some research.[2]

Consider how recent statistics show that when it comes to morality and lifestyle issues, there is little difference between the behavior (and one can assume condition of the heart) of Christians and non-Christians.

Divorce rates are about the same.

The percentages of men who regularly view pornography are roughly the same — and it's a lot of men.

Christians are considered to be more than two times as likely to have racist attitudes as non-Christians.

Domestic violence, drug and alcohol abuse, and most other problems are just as prevalent among Christians as among non-Christians.

Consider too statistics about evangelicals. About one in four people living together outside marriage call themselves evangelicals.

Only about 6 percent of evangelicals regularly tithe.

Only about half the people who say they regularly attend church actually do. And a significant number of younger adults (millennials) believe that evangelical churches are not even Christlike or Christian. Sixty to 80 percent of young people will leave the church in their twenties.[3]

Fewer than one out of five who claim to be born-again Christians have a worldview of even a few fundamental biblical beliefs. Plenty of people call themselves Christians, but very few people can actually tell you what it means—from the Bible's perspective—to be a Christian. They might call themselves Christians, but they also believe that the Bible is full of errors or that God is not one God manifest in three persons or that Jesus Christ did not lead a sinless life (or that he isn't God) or that simply being good will get you into heaven.

When you ask most evangelicals what their job as a believer is, they may tell you that they are to share Christ, but how many actually do? At worst, they follow the rule that you don't talk about politics and religion, and they will die without ever seeing anyone come to faith. At best, they may invite people to church, but they think making disciples is not their job; it's the pastor's job.

We could go on and on. One can't help but conclude that something is wrong. Where's the lasting life change? Where are the transformed lives? Why are people in our churches just like the world? Why are we not developing people who are Christlike?

A few years back, Bill Hybels, pastor of Willow Creek Church, one of the most influential churches in America, revealed the results of a months-long study into the church's effectiveness. The conclusion was that the church simply wasn't producing the results they were hoping for. Willow Creek's leaders did research into other churches across the country and came to the same conclusions.[4] In the foreword to *Reveal*, a book outlining their discoveries, Bill Hybels wrote, "The local church is the hope of the world. For a number of years now, I have shared this message whenever I've had the opportunity to serve pastors of local churches across the nation and around the world. It's a message I believe with all my heart. So you can imagine my reaction when three people whose counsel I value told me that the local church I've been the pastor of for more than three decades was not doing as well as we thought when it came to spiritual growth. As if that wasn't bad enough, they said this wasn't just their opinion. It was based on scientific research."[5]

The results rocked Willow Creek's world. Willow Creek's leaders realized that they had to make significant changes. Hybels put it this way: "Our dream is that we fundamentally change the way we do church. That we take out a clean sheet of paper and we rethink all of our old assumptions. Replace it with new insights. Insights that are informed by research and rooted in Scripture. Our dream is really to discover what God is doing and how he's asking us to transform this planet."[6]

That's what's required of us as well. To be effective, we need to make a fundamental shift in the way we do church. What we're doing now isn't working, at least not like we'd hoped. We have defined ourselves by emphases and methodologies that don't produce results.

Fortunately, there is hope ahead. Within the pages of God's Word is a design that will lead to effectiveness. The solution to our ineffectiveness as churches involves following a clear and uncomplicated way to train people to be spiritually mature, fully devoted followers of Christ, and then in turn having those disciples make more disciples.

What we need in our churches today are fewer "Christians," at least in today's popular definition of the word. Now, I don't want fewer saved people. Far from it. I want as many to be saved as possible. But the point is that fewer than we think are actually saved.

What I want are full-fledged followers of Jesus Christ, and to produce that in our churches today, we need a radical shift. We need more of the engine that Jesus used to change the world, the engine he instructs us to use. This engine will not create perfect churches, but it will create *effective* churches.

It's relational discipleship.

Ask Dr. Coleman

Is the church today doing its job to the degree that it could?

As church leaders, we definitely need to ask ourselves whether our churches are as effective as they could be. I'm afraid, however, that the church is not living up to her potential.

The church is preserving itself well, content to maintain a rearguard action, content to protect the status quo. But that's not what God has called the church to do. God wants the church to do more than merely hold its own. We're in a battle against the powers and principalities of this world. Aggressive action is needed.

Regrettably, I've seen a lack of effectiveness all too often. It leaves you with a sinking feeling to see what great potential there is in a person or a church, yet to see them settling for second or third best. It leaves you with the feeling of sorrow. American poet and abolitionist John Greenleaf Whittier said, "For all sad words of tongue and pen, / The saddest are these, 'It might have been.' "

There are, however, many exciting places in the world today where the church is moving. I think of the Covenant Evangelical Free Church in Singapore. More than 4,500 people fill the five Sunday services on two campuses, and a third campus soon will be under construction. Twenty-five years ago when Edmund Chan, fresh out of college, became a pastor, his discouraged congregation had only seventeen members. But this gifted expositor of Scripture had a vision to make disciples who truly worship God in all arenas of life by the enabling of the Spirit. He began to train men who would take up their crosses and follow Christ, teaching them to train others to live the same lifestyle. It was radical discipleship. As the church multiplied, so did its outreach in missions and church planting around the world. When I visited the church in the spring of 2012, a spirit of revival pervaded the atmosphere. I call that a church alive, a church living in the fulfillment of the Great Commission.

A church like this gives me hope. Today's churches need constantly to strive through the power of the Holy Spirit to be as effective as they can be.

The solution to our ineffectiveness as churches is to train people to be spiritually mature, fully devoted followers of Christ, and then in turn to have those disciples make more disciples.

FOUR MAIN CATEGORIES

How did the church get to the state it's in today? Simply put, the problem stems from the way today's churches are designed. Within North America, each local church is characterized by two important components.

The first is *focus*. Think of a church's focus as the primary emphasis that it commits its time and resources to achieve. It's the engine that drives everything else in that church. For instance, a church may desire to reach lost people, so it will expend its energy and resources on bridge events and worship services focused on giving reasons to believe and issuing invitations to accept and follow Christ.

The second component is *methodology*. This is the way a church sets itself up systematically to accomplish its purpose, or the manner in which it tries to achieve its focus. It could also be thought of as a structure or a system environment (as we call it in the sports world) that a church has created to accomplish what it values.

Every church has its focus and its methodology for achieving its focus whether it realizes it or not. When looking at the different kinds of churches, leaders disagree over how many categories of churches exist today. Some hold that there are only two main categories — attractional and missional. Others add a third — organic (sometimes called "house"). Others add a fourth — educational. The disagreement stems mainly from crossover and blending of focus and methodologies. Truly, most churches don't fit any category exactly. Nevertheless, I find that most churches today will lean toward one of the following four categories, even if a category doesn't fit precisely.

Category 1: Educational

A pastoral-educational focus with a classroom methodology.

In the educational category, a church uses the bulk of its energy on biblical education, and it's understood that the pastor's job (along with the pastoral staff) is to provide this education for the people. Leaders and members make well-intentioned statements such as, "We believe the Bible is God's Word, and we want to get it into the heads of our people." Churches with this emphasis focus on Bible study and doctrine.

The methodology in these churches is most often the classroom model. A strong emphasis is placed on Sunday morning teaching times, Sunday school attendance, perhaps a midweek educational forum, youth and children's programs and Bible studies, and perhaps information-oriented teacher-led small groups.

Sometimes a strong emphasis is placed on pastoral care as well, though few churches, especially larger churches, are intentional about this aspect. The paid, formally trained, professional pastors are responsible for developing and implementing programs for teaching Bible knowledge. The pastors in churches where care is expected are also responsible for caring for the congregants, so heavy expectations are placed on the pastors' time. Congregants want pastors to visit them in the hospital, counsel them, open meetings with prayer, attend myriad planning meetings, drop everything to come to their aid in family crises, and seldom take time off for vacation (otherwise, who will lead the church?).

The educational model typically doesn't stress attracting new people to the church as much as it does educating and taking care of people who are already there. Those who come through the door expect to be biblically educated, and this is often (in their minds) the meaning of "becoming a mature disciple." The hope is that the education will translate to Christian behavior outside the walls of the church.

Category 2: Attractional

An attractional focus with an entertainment methodology.

The well-meaning emphasis in the attractional category is placed on biblical evangelism through church services and large events that attract people. Helping people to "make decisions for Christ" is primary. It is assumed that discipleship will happen through church attendance. Some churches in this category seek to retain people who have attended church for years in more traditional settings, by updating the way songs are sung and lessons are taught. The modern way of doing things tends to keep people from being bored with church, at least for a while. The key is to design church services to win people.

In this category, people are attracted to the church because they have real questions and hurts that need answering and dealing with. The sermons are designed to answer those questions and address those hurts. The leaders in these churches are focused on taking ground outside the walls of the church by using the weekend service as a hook. They really seek to inspire Christians to invite their friends to the services where an invitation to accept Christ is given. Worship services are usually professional and celebratory in nature, limited in depth, and will sometimes use non-Christian music to identify with the church's primary demographic—unsaved people. Good coffee is served. Dress is casual. Messages are shorter, practical, and relational in style.

Category 3: Missional

A missional focus with a service-opportunity methodology.

Churches in the missional category are sometimes referred to as social justice churches. The focus is biblical action. These churches are designed around the paradigm in which God has given each person a kingdom-oriented purpose, and each person needs to discover that purpose and then live it out in practical, tangible, community-changing ways.

The methodology is service. Christians are primarily encouraged to become active outside their church's walls for the purpose of social change and as a means of "living out Christ's kingdom."

The church might encourage its people, for instance, to focus on feeding the homeless or working in a women's shelter. People might organize community cleanup days in the name of Jesus, or anonymously leave packets of diapers on the doorsteps of young mothers. People might be encouraged to live radically and simply, focusing on others rather than possessions.

Missional churches are typically contemporary in style, but not always. Some are more liturgical. Some are traditional yet have a strong, driving sense of outreach.

Category 4: Organic or "Home"

A fellowship focus with an organic methodology.

In the organic category, the emphasis is biblical relationships, or fellowship. These churches focus on Bible verses that talk about how people need to be devoted to each other in brotherly love and close fellowship.

The methodology used is home groups (sometimes called "house churches"). In this model, a group of believers might gather together in an informal, relational way for teaching, worship, service, and fellowship, yet there would be very little organizational structure involved. They would hold few or no regular public, large group services and may not have any main meeting place other than the homes they live in. (Though I am aware of several churches in this model that like to meet as a whole once a month in a rented facility.)

They might initiate activities to serve their communities, but the emphasis is placed on the home group doing the service, rather than attracting people into the house church. The main emphasis is "doing life together," or journeying together as people who love God and are devoted to him.

Your church may fit precisely into one of these categories. Or it might straddle two or more of them. Your church might believe in all or some of the church functions that these categories represent, but it probably focuses on one and hopes the others will happen naturally. That's okay. Think of these categories as broad brushstrokes that help to provide definitions.

THE COMMON ELEMENT: SOMETHING'S MISSING

Please note that my purpose is never to bash any other churches. Rather, I want to enter into the struggles these other churches are facing. In the Relational Discipleship Network training sessions, we work with churches in each of these categories every month, so we get to see and hear firsthand what is working and what isn't. The churches are led by people who love the Lord, but the leaders know and articulate that something is missing. To be clear, there is much to commend in all four models. None are intrinsically wrong, and leaders of each model can use proof texts to create biblical reasons for what they do. Plus, there are pockets of effectiveness in each model—even tremendous effectiveness for a period of time.

But there are also tremendous challenges with each. Again, we must ask if any of these models are truly succeeding. Are people being transformed from spiritual immaturity to maturity, and are they following Jesus in regular, lasting, and effective ways? The answer, according to the statistics we referred to earlier, is sometimes yes and sometimes no. But mostly, unfortunately, no.

The common element in the four categories of churches is that the models are incomplete. The focus and the methodologies are improperly placed, in such a way that there are missing components that leave the church one-dimensional, when it was meant to be complete. That only causes problems in the long run. That's what we're aiming to shift.

For instance, in an educational model, one of the greatest challenges is pastoral burnout if the pastor is expected to teach and care for all the people in relational ways. I've talked with pastors operating in this model who tell how they get so caught up in creating sermons, making sure all the programs are running, and caring for all the perceived needs of the church that they are continually exhausted. The expectations placed on church leaders in this model are sky-high, impossible to fulfill. Those in this category also have a very real problem with effectiveness even in the area of real learning. Usually people who go to these churches love to listen to the pastor speak and become very reliant upon him and his understanding rather than learning to understand the Bible for themselves. When they do read themselves, it just isn't as interesting as when they hear it from the master teacher. Also, lecturing is the least effective way to teach anything and leads to few really understanding the truth that the teacher wants them to understand. Because the teacher cannot unpack what he is teaching in practical ways, the people often have wrong understandings of how to apply the truth. They can misrepresent or misunderstand what the teacher really believes or would do in any given situation in the real world of their everyday lives.

Similarly, I've spoken with pastors of attractional churches who describe how their church succeeds in bringing people in and helping them make decisions for Jesus but leaves those people in a spiritual childlike state in which, over time, they conclude that their needs aren't being met. Or they decide that maybe Jesus isn't real because they were not taught what to expect from a relationship with God. When trouble comes, they don't know what to do or why bad things happen, and then the enemy comes and does what he always does—causes doubt and conflict. The people drift away from the faith or get frustrated and angry and stick around causing problems. Or they'll leave and go to a church with an educational model so they can go deeper in their faith (or so they think).

There is much good in the missional model, yet I've spoken with pastors who describe similar frustrations. They note that if mission to the poor and marginalized is the primary focus of a church, then they always have people giving and reaching out, but not much is being invested back; there is not enough that builds the believers up. A missional church will grow, but since its focus is primarily on doing things for hurting people (who will continually take), eventually the people will burn out, particularly if service and action aren't balanced with the rest of life. When a church is focused on doing things for other people, then the problem is either that the people receiving the service aren't very appreciative or that the intrinsic acts of service don't yield a lot of fruit. There's no sustaining strength that comes from relationship with other believers.

People who interact with the organic model tell how a church focused on doing life together has its strengths for sure, but if they are not careful, it too can get out of balance. Spending time with people can grow very frustrating unless the people you are doing life with are becoming more and more like Jesus. If not, eventually these people get irritated with each other or hurt each other and move on. God's idea of real relationship includes being together, yes, but while we are together, we are being transparent and authentic with a goal—to become a disciple of Jesus who can make disciples of Jesus. A strict emphasis on fellowship alone creates a church that struggles with an inward focus instead of reaching others, because the group values real relationships that require so much. This makes it hard to include newcomers, especially lost people. I've heard participants in this movement describe how at some point this church model has a tendency to become cliquish, dysfunctional, even cultish. Limited new lifeblood comes into this church, and it often implodes or disbands.

What's the solution, then? If the purpose of a church is not primarily to transfer information, if it's not primarily to attract people, if it's not primarily to serve our communities, and if it's not primarily to encourage fellowship, why then does the church exist? All four functions are important components of a church, but none should be the main focus of a church—not as Jesus defined it, anyway.

So what is the main focus of the church supposed to be?

DISCIPLESHIP, NOT EVANGELISM

A solution emerges when a church shifts its focus to biblical discipleship using the methodology of relational environments. In the chapters to come, we'll talk in depth about what this means, but notice those two key words again in relation to what we're espousing, and keep the ideas in mind so you can begin to chew on them.

Focus = biblical discipleship

Methodology = relational environments

We believe that discipleship should be the core focus for the church. And we believe that the relational model Jesus utilized is the timeless and best methodology for discipleship. The "relational discipleship model" embraces all aspects of the main four categories, yet it espouses something different as the one driving focus.

This model doesn't measure success by how many people come to a church, how much money is given, or even how many converts are made. These things are worth measuring, but they're always secondary. The model we advocate measures success by how many people are being loved and led into the way of Jesus, are coming to Christ and following him. It measures how many people are being transformed into Christ's likeness and are pursuing his kingdom mission. It values and measures how many are actually becoming disciples who can make disciples.

Let's start with the question of focus. As mentioned, one problem today is that churches are full of "Christians" but not disciples, and yes, there is a significant difference. In the early church, the first followers of Jesus were called disciples. Later they were called Christians because of their association with Christ (Acts 11:26). But the Bible never instructs us to make Christians, not in today's loose sense of the word, in which more than 80 percent of Americans claim to be Christian.[7] The Bible refers to disciples around 270 times, but to Christians just three times. So a focus on discipleship is the first overall shift with which we must grapple.

Consider how the New Testament is intensely Christ-centered. Jesus is the key to everything else. He is the Bread of Life, the Light of the World, the Good Shepherd, the Vine, the Gate, the Way, Truth, and Life, and the model to follow. The ideal life is focused on Jesus. It is not just trusting him but also truly following him. To focus on him is to live a fulfilling life. It is about becoming more and more like him in the power of the Holy Spirit to the glory of God. To be conformed into Jesus' likeness is the goal (Rom. 8:29). The word for this is *discipleship*. The New Testament church was all about being and making disciples of Jesus.

DeYoung and Gilbert's comprehensive study *What Is the Mission of the Church?* deals with many of the complicated questions about the mission or purpose of the church that thoughtful people are asking. My coauthors and I have found their book to be a helpful one because it deals comprehensively with all the biblical material. We could not recommend it more highly, especially to young leaders. They sum it all up in a simple statement: "The mission of the church—your church, my church, the church in Appalachia, the church in Azerbaijan, the church anywhere—is to make disciples of Jesus Christ in the power of the Spirit to the glory of God the Father."[8]

New Testament scholar Michael Wilkins puts it this way: "Since all true Christians are disciples, the ministry of the church may be seen in its broadest sense as 'discipleship.' Various ministries within the church should be seen as specialization, aspects, or stages of discipleship training."[9]

Let's focus on a key text that can help us with this point, the Great Commission (Matt. 28:18 – 20). Too many churches refer to this passage in the sense of making converts only. But that line of thinking ignores both the meaning of the word *disciple* and the phrases in the text that define what is involved in making disciples. Let's look carefully at what it says: "Jesus came and said to them, 'All authority in heaven and on earth has been given to me. Go therefore and *make disciples* of all nations, baptizing them in the name of the Father and of the Son and of the Holy Spirit, teaching them to observe all that I have commanded you. And behold, I am with you always, to the end of the age'" (ESV, emphasis added).

All authority was given to Jesus. He commanded his disciples to go and make disciples. Disciples are not merely converts but also doers, learners, students, Christ followers, or better yet, "apprentices of Jesus."[10] We make disciples, the text tells us, by baptizing people who respond to the gospel message and by teaching them to obey everything Jesus commanded.[11] So notice Jesus tells us that he has all authority, and then he tells us to teach what he commanded. So it is right to say that following Christ is a nonnegotiable part of the Great Commission.

To be clear, the call isn't to perfection. A disciple of Jesus will be imperfect, even as Peter denied Christ, Thomas doubted Christ, and many other disciples misunderstood Christ. Yet the call of a true disciple is a call to a change in allegiance, from self to Jesus' leadership in our lives. In a disciple's life, the Great Commission must be taken at face value. If anyone serves Jesus, he *must* follow Jesus. There is no wiggle room in a genuine Christian's life for a faith characterized by compromise.

Jesus not only told us to make disciples but also gave us a model to follow in doing so. I believe that most Christians have divorced the teachings of Jesus from the methods of Jesus, and yet they expect the results of Jesus. I believe his methods are just as divine as his teachings. He showed us that the fundamental methodology in making disciples is relationships grounded in truth and love. Jesus is the greatest disciple maker in history, and his way works. Discipleship is the emphasis. Relationships are the method. Jesus invited people into relationships with himself; he loved them and in the process showed them how to follow God. His primary method was life-on-life.

The method Jesus used with his disciples was the same method that the Old Testament advocated for parents to use to disciple their children. Deuteronomy 6:5 – 9 states it succinctly: "You shall love the LORD your God with all your heart and with all your soul and with all your might. And these words that I command you today shall be on your heart. You shall teach them diligently to your children, and shall talk of them when you sit in your house, and when you walk by the way, and when you lie down, and when you rise. You shall bind them as a sign on your hand, and they shall be as frontlets between your eyes. You shall write them on the doorposts of your house and on your gates" (ESV).

Parents were to equip their children to love and obey God. The method was relationship ("when you sit in your house," "when you walk by the way," and "when you lie down"). And the whole process was discipleship, or in today's language, apprenticeship.

It is spiritual parenting.[12] In the Gospels, this method is seen when Jesus invited people into his life. He picked twelve to be his disciples, with the goal that they would carry on his ministry when he left. He invested in them by talking to them when they sat down, when they walked along the road, and when they laid down.

The apostle Paul and others also used this same method. Consider

2 Timothy 3:10–14, where Paul describes his relationship with Timothy: "You, however, have followed my teaching, my conduct, my aim in life, my faith, my patience, my love, my steadfastness, my persecutions and sufferings that happened to me at Antioch, at Iconium, and at Lystra.... Continue in what you have learned and have firmly believed, knowing from whom you learned it" (ESV).

Paul didn't simply lead a Sunday school class once a week or preach a sermon to a large crowd and end there. He focused on doing life with people he discipled. In the Bible, relationships are the context and environment for discipleship. It was the way of parents and many leaders in the Old Testament; it was the way of Paul and the apostles in the New Testament; but most important, it was the method of Jesus.

Jesus' method is the best one for the church moving forward. It can be called "intentional relational discipleship." And this book explains how you can implement this method at every level of the local church.

STORIES OF EFFECTIVENESS

To close this first chapter, I asked my friend Jerry Harris, senior pastor of The Crossing, in Quincy, Illinois, to share about what making the shift to the relational discipleship model was like for his church, as well as some stories he's seen of effective discipleship in action in his church.

Jerry's church, previously known as Payson Road Christian Church, is an independent, nondenominational church started in 1970, and a good example of an established church that has made the shift to the relational discipleship model in recent years.

Today the church has grown to more than four thousand people in six locations, and Jerry consistently reports strong levels of growth and spiritual maturity in his members.

Jerry wrote,

Over the years, we had become building dependent, staff dependent, and technology dependent. Most of our structure depended on attracting new people, using these three components. I was fairly certain that if our building no longer existed, our church wouldn't either.

I visited Jim Putman at Real Life and saw that his church was built a different way. All the emphasis was placed on discipleship primarily happening in small groups. He even said that if there had to be a choice, he would prefer his people attending their small group instead of weekend worship. All of this was hitting me sideways.

Small groups have always been more of a necessary chore than a great opportunity to me. I had always seen them more in terms of a program than anything else. It has always been difficult to get them going and even harder to keep them going.

Yet here I was, visiting a church with over eight hundred small groups. Real Life was making it work without much concern at all for attraction.

I recoiled from Jim's insistence on the primacy of discipleship and felt myself continually backed into corners. "You're a flock shooter, Jerry," he said, evaluating The Crossing approach. "A flock shooter is a lousy hunter with a gun and no plan. When the flock is scared into flight, he just shoots as many rounds as he can into the flock, hoping he'll hit something. Usually he just wounds a few, if he hits them at all. But a good hunter picks out a bird, leads it, and pulls the trigger."

Jim was right. He was saying that our approach — preaching to the crowd — was like shooting the Word of God into the congregation and hoping that we hit something. It wasn't the way that Jesus did it or the way the early church operated.

Jesus got far more accomplished through twelve committed guys than he did with any of the large crowds he attracted. As Jim began to explain to me a different and better way of discipleship, I began to realize how we had missed the mark.

The recognition of how far our church and the church in general was from Jesus' method was a hard pill to swallow, but if real change was going to happen, then the senior leader had to swallow it first. I decided that change began with me, even if it was hard.

Making the shift with our church took vision, courage, time, and energy. But the results in years since have been highly worth it. We wanted to keep attracting, but we became intentional about what happened next. Our focus had to change — we had to pour

our energy into building a system that would enable people to do life with more mature people who would help them grow. It meant a lot of change, but the change led to a movement in our area that extended outside our walls.

Let me tell you the background of several of our present staff. For instance, The Crossing met Billy while he was in the psychiatric unit of a hospital in our area. He was dangerous to himself and losing his battle because of his addiction to meth.

Because of the relational discipleship focus of Celebrate Recovery (CR) at our church, a couple of our guys invested in Billy. They did more than bring him to church and lead him in the CR small group. They met with him in restaurants and talked to him when he was tempted or confused or frustrated. They taught him how to live and love by giving him a model to follow. Billy began to find personal victory over his addiction. Before long, Billy was leading CR groups and working as a volunteer at the church. As his mentor saw Billy's increased stability, he recommended him for a custodial job at the church. Billy was now surrounding himself with friends and former addicts, discipling them through recovery and going through small group leader training.

Billy is now a critically positive spiritual force in many lives, reproducing himself over and over again in areas where many of us would be simply clueless. A nondiscipling church would struggle with raising up people like Billy into any productive role, let alone a key role.

Chris was raised in church but fell out of it pretty early. A few years ago he was managing a local restaurant. A drug-addicted wife whom he had divorced had complicated his life, but he continued to raise their two children. He met his present wife while they were both employed at the restaurant. She encouraged him to come to church with her, but he put up a fight.

Chris's decision to join her began to reveal God's plan for him. He developed a relationship with the leader of our children's ministry, who poured into him while using him as a volunteer in his ministry. When that minister transitioned to the mission field, the next children's minister continued mentoring and could see Chris as an assistant.

Eventually Chris transitioned into the role of children's minister, affecting the lives of both children and parents. Chris sees the family as God's perfect example of relational discipleship and today is transitioning to direct all the small groups at one of our campuses.

I met George about ten years ago when he moved back to town and started attending The Crossing. He was making a six-figure salary working as a regional sales manager for a national company. He had a business degree and had owned or run businesses over the years.

In his midforties, success was starting to give way to a desire for significance. He had been a high-functioning alcoholic for many years and was in recovery. His past addiction and lifestyle had blown him through a lot of money and three marriages.

Jim (not Jim Putman) came forward in a church service broken and repentant. He wanted deep change but needed godly men around him to coach him. Dick stepped up, inviting Jim to his small group and mentoring him daily. Jim started seeing himself from God's point of view and started hungering for opportunities in ministry.

Because of the efforts of mentors who poured into Jim, he is now campus pastor at one of our locations and has reproduced himself over and over.

Wayne came to The Crossing with a serious, even dangerous temper problem that had torn apart his marriage. His anger and bitterness was always looking for a target. One of those targets had been his wife. I can remember counseling Wayne and seeing the unsettling look in his eyes.

Jim began discipling Wayne, just doing life with him, helping him to navigate through all of his accumulated junk.

Today Wayne is one of our small group trainers working alongside Jim, training our pastors and leaders, and one of the sweetest and gentlest spirits at The Crossing.

Those are the stories we want to see in churches all across the world today, stories of God transforming people through the methodology of relational discipleship.

The overarching shift to begin thinking about is that churches are not called to merely make converts or even "Christians," in the limited sense of the word. Churches have tried that, and it's not producing the intended results. Churches must begin moving to a model of church that champions biblical discipleship in relational environments. Simply put, a church exists to make *disciples who make disciples*. And the primary methodology is Christlike love expressed in life-on-life *relationship*.

But how? What are the specific shifts that need to happen?

Once you have the overarching shift in mind, we recommend five further specific shifts, and the first begins with defusing a potential powder keg. More about this in the next chapter.

KEY POINTS

- The core question of effectiveness — the question that ultimately matters — is whether the people getting saved are being conformed into the likeness of Christ (Col. 1:28).
- The solution is to train people to be spiritually mature, fully devoted followers of Christ, and then in turn to have those disciples make more disciples.
- The four main models of churches today are incomplete. The emphases and the methodologies are missing components that leave the church one-dimensional.
- We must become disciple-making churches, and that happens best in *relational* environments. A small group that meets solely for the sake of relationships misses the point. But relationships that exist for the purpose of discipleship mature people spiritually.

SHIFT

1

From Reaching
to Making

Chapter 2

DEFINING A DISCIPLE

What does it mean to be a disciple of Jesus?

Anytime you gather a group of people to accomplish a goal, you first need to get everyone on the same page. You need to define what you want to accomplish and how you are going to do it.

Picture a football team. When the quarterback gathers the other players in a huddle and calls out, "Slant 86, double cross 99 right," every other player needs to know what play the quarterback is talking about and the part they are to play in it. Otherwise, when the huddle breaks, and they get set at the line of scrimmage, and the ball is snapped, it's just chaos on the field.

This same principle is true

- For sailors navigating a ship.
- For workers assembling cars at a factory.
- For soldiers advancing on the enemy.
- For a band playing music.

Whenever any group sets out to work together to accomplish a goal, the tasks, methods, and objectives need to be defined, clearly communicated, and understood by everyone involved.

Have you applied this commonsense principle to your church? In your gut-level-honest times of self-assessment, is every leader in your church on the same page? Do they all agree on what success looks like?

A POTENTIAL POWDER KEG

Church leaders frequently come as a team to our training seminars at Real Life Ministries. We encourage the pastors, staff, and elders to work together as they progress through the training. In the past, one of the first exercises we'd go through is to ask each team two assessment questions. They had to answer these questions as individuals, writing them down on a piece of paper, without discussing their answers with the rest of their group. We then asked them to give their answers to the person facilitating the group.

The first question we asked is simple: "What's the purpose of the church?"

Since this is a training seminar about discipleship, most everyone would already have that idea in mind — *discipleship*. Or they'd add some caveats and clarifications to this answer, emphasizing a specific area of church they championed or worked in. An evangelism pastor would write something like, "The purpose of the church is to reach our community for the glory of God so we can make disciples." A worship pastor would add, "We need good worship that captures the attention of the lost who may come to a weekend service."

The second question was a bit more difficult for them to answer ... and I'll tell you what it is in just a minute. But first you need to understand that *how* each person answers this second question is crucial to the exercise. We asked individuals on the team to write their answers down anonymously, because this reveals what people really think about their church. The second question, in particular, can be dangerous because it surfaces different understandings about what the team believes they have agreed upon. In other cases it reveals that each group may be frustrated by the rest of their teammates because they, in their minds, have not done their job. Sometimes, even if you can't see it from the outside, a church leadership team is sitting on a powder keg. The fuse has been lit, and it is quickly burning.

So what is this second question? It's the next logical question to ask! Since most of the teams have come to agree that the purpose of a church is discipleship (or something close to it), we followed up that question by asking, "What is a disciple?" In all our years of asking this question, we encountered only two churches in which the entire team of leaders agreed on the same definition.

This second question brings the team face-to-face with the heart of their purpose and values as a church. Below, we've listed several definitions we commonly see. As you read these examples, ask yourself how members of *your* church's leadership might answer this question. Also think through what problems can be created if everyone has a different definition of a mature disciple.

- A disciple of Jesus is a person who is becoming spiritually mature. This occurs when a Christian knows his Bible inside and out. That's what's most important in our church: knowing the Bible.
- A disciple is a person who cares for the lost. He regularly invites his friends, neighbors, and unsaved family members to our church so they can hear about Jesus. That's what's most important: getting people in the door of the church so they hear the good news! We want to make the weekend events as understandable to the lost and immature as we can.
- A disciple is a person who is doing life with others. He has made all he has available to others in the sphere of relationships. He is focused on working together in a small group to serve some need in the community. He wants to right a wrong in the culture in the name of Jesus.
- A disciple is a person who loves the poor and marginalized in Jesus' name. We live and love like Jesus lived and loved. That means we're especially kind, compassionate, and tolerant to everybody we meet. That's what's most important: love wins!
- A disciple is a person who has come to understand what righteousness is and is being sanctified so that he lives differently in the world. He abstains from sin and loves the Word of God.
- A mature disciple worships God with his or her resources and energy. They want to know God and make him known. The worship of God is central to a mature believer's life.
- A mature disciple is a witness for Christ in every way. He knows how to win someone to Jesus and participates in sharing his or her faith as individuals and as a part of the local church.

All of these answers sound good, even biblical, at least on the surface. Often the people who write them are passionate, well-meaning, educated Christians who want their churches to be as effective as possible. But big problems begin to arise when a church doesn't agree on its basic definitions, direction, and philosophy of ministry. One staff member will want to champion Bible trivia nights so people will learn the Bible in a fun way, while another believes adding great-tasting coffee in the foyer is the ticket to success. Another will want to establish a mission for the homeless, while others will want to emphasize the importance of church members spending more time hanging out with their unsaved neighbors. Some will want to host large evangelistic outreach events, while others will want to gather together as believers in their homes so they can really get to know each other.

It's essential for the leadership of a church to have a unified understanding of their goal and purpose as a church. And it's equally important that they have a unified methodology to accomplish that goal. You need everyone on the same page. But how?

Let's go to God's Word.

Ask / Dr. Coleman

What's the difference between making converts and making disciples?

A church must correctly define *disciple* before it can move toward making disciples.

Conversion is the first step in the discipleship process. A convert is one who turns around. Meaning, a person is moving one direction, becomes convicted of sin, turns the other direction, and comes to Christ. By simple faith, the person receives the gift of salvation. Conversion is the beginning of a journey, whereas discipleship is ongoing.

In true conversion, a person must commit to following Jesus. The person becomes a lifelong learner, a disciple. Being a disciple is a learning process that never ends. Thankfully, I think it will go on into heaven. I don't think we'll ever finish learning, since we're finite and God is infinite. That's one of the things that will make heaven exciting—we'll continue to discover more of the riches of the grace of God.

In a sense, a person can be a disciple even before he is converted. I might call that a "pre-disciple," although I don't think we need to get technical about it.

The problem today is that our churches are full of converts.

So the question we must answer is, How do we disciple converts?

DEFINING A DISCIPLE

There are two practical criteria that must guide any proposed definition of a disciple. First, the definition needs to be *biblical* (as Jesus defined it), and second, it needs to be *clear*. What we're aiming for is a definition that every leader in our church understands and operates by, so we don't want a complicated definition that no one can remember. At the same time, we don't want to leave out something that Jesus taught. So it must be simple enough that a child can understand but as complex as it was meant to be. Think of the definition as a map on the wall. It's visible, accessible, and easy to comprehend.

Often people ask me how I define what a disciple is, and I point them to Jesus' statement in Matthew 4:19: "He [Jesus] said to them, 'Follow me, and I will make you fishers of men'" (ESV).

I like to say that in this invitation to the disciples was the definition as Jesus saw it. It's a simple verse, and everybody in our leadership knows it. But why Matthew 4:19? Why not some other verse? Certainly, there are other places in Scripture where a church can turn to define what it means to be a disciple. Our goal is not to create a one-size-fits-all definition based on a single proof text. At Real

Life, we have decided to use this simple verse because it serves as an outline. While it doesn't say everything that needs to be said about being a disciple, it is broad enough and simple enough to be supported by other Scriptures that detail the life of a maturing disciple. Your church may well opt to use a different text to define discipleship, and that's fine. Just make sure your definition is biblical and clear and that your people are speaking the same language.

THREE KEY ATTRIBUTES

Jesus says the words of Matthew 4:19 to two brothers, Peter and Andrew, while they are casting a net beside the Sea of Galilee. In the most basic sense, his invitation is specific to these two men — men who worked as first-century fishermen. But the invitation Jesus makes to Peter and Andrew is also a more general invitation, one that he gives to each of us as well.

If we dig into this verse as a framework and model for understanding discipleship, we find three important attributes of a disciple.

1. "Follow Me"

The first two words of Jesus are a simple invitation. This invitation indicates our acceptance of Jesus — his authority and his truth — at the *head* level.

Jesus said, "Follow me."

A disciple of Jesus must follow Jesus.

It's that simple. Jesus leads. We follow.

Following means that we recognize and accept who Jesus is as Lord, leader, and master of our lives. He's the one who initiates and guides. In turn, we respond to his leadership and direction. Following Jesus means acknowledging that Jesus is in front and we must place ourselves behind him. John 12:26 speaks of this process: "Whoever serves me must follow me; and where I am, my servant also will be."

Some people are taught that when they accept Jesus as their leader and Lord, he will fulfill all of their wishes and their plans for their lives. But this is simply not true. In Jesus' definition, a disciple is someone who *knows* him (who he is and what he is like) and *follows* him. Though we used to be self-ruled, now we are Christ-ruled. John 14:23–24 connects our obedience to Christ to our hearts and affections: "Anyone who loves me will obey my teaching. My Father will love them, and we will come to them and make our home with them. Anyone who does not love me will not obey my teaching." A willingness to follow Jesus is evidence of our love for him, and though our obedience to Jesus is not perfect (Heb. 12:1), it should be evident and growing.

When we answer the call to follow Jesus, we are not shown the specific route to our destination. Nor are we promised that the journey will be easy. In fact, Matthew 16:24–26 uses strong language to tell us that a follower of Jesus must deny himself, take up his cross, and lose his life in the process of gaining the life Jesus offers. Yet as difficult as the journey may be, people who follow Jesus are also given important promises. Jesus promises that those who follow him will never be abandoned. He tells us that he will always be with us, even to the very end of the age (Matt. 28:20).

Though the notion of obeying Jesus is connected to our hearts at some level, this first attribute of a disciple is primarily a *mental acceptance* of Jesus, understanding that he is now the one in charge of our lives. He is the boss, our leader. The invitation to follow him speaks to us at the head level. When people make a decision to follow Jesus, at some level they must first know and accept who he is, even if they don't fully grasp all that will be required of them as a disciple.[13] Of course, we want to acknowledge that there are actions, emotions, and affections involved with this decision as well. We are not arguing that each of these happens apart from the others. We are simply pointing out that all three of these unique elements must be present. Jesus lovingly rules our lives, and as he does, he replaces the falsehood we were handed from the world with the truth. He is a light that illuminates our thinking, and we move from foolishness to wisdom as we spend time with him and his Word, the source of truth and wisdom. The invitation to follow means learning and believing truths about Jesus. This leads to change at the headship (authority) and head (knowledge) level.

2. "And I Will Make You"

The next five words in this verse speak of a process of transformation. This tells us that discipleship involves Jesus molding our *hearts* to become more like his. Jesus invites us to follow him and says he will make us into fishers of men. In other words, a disciple of Jesus is *changed* by Jesus. Not only must we make a mental decision to follow Christ; there must also be a process of transformation in which a work takes place in our heart and affections.

After Jesus invites Peter and Andrew to follow him, he hints at what he's going to do. We know from other passages of Scripture that disciples of Jesus are changed by Jesus, through the power of his Holy Spirit.[14] He transforms his disciples into something new, people who are different than they were when they first met him and started following him. Romans 8:29 tells us that we are being conformed into the image of Christ. Second Corinthians 3:17–18 promises us that God is transforming us from one degree of glory into another into this image.

This is important for us to remember, because we mistakenly forget that God is ultimately the one who invites us to be his disciple even before any change is ever made in us. We wrongly assume that people must clean up their lives before coming to Jesus. We then also get discouraged once we have accepted the invitation because we often fail in many ways. We think that God's grace covered us up to the point of salvation and somehow we must now get it right to continue as Jesus' disciple. If we read the Gospels and study the disciples of Jesus, we find that they often acted in ways that were selfish, rude, clueless, and immature. They were not spiritual giants; they were just regular guys with the same selfish, sinful struggles we all have. Jesus didn't choose them to be his followers because they were anything special. He chose them with an eye to who they could become. Responding to the call to follow Jesus meant allowing him to unmake them and then remake them into his image—as his disciples.

Note the transforming work that takes place in the disciples' lives. In John 15:1–2, Jesus says, "I am the true vine, and my Father is the gardener. He cuts off every branch in me that bears no fruit, while every branch that does bear fruit he prunes so that it will be even more fruitful." In times of pruning, we are tempted to leave Jesus. We think he is failing to affirm us as we are, and we're right—he's actually shaping us into something else, something better. All the while, he has counted us as righteous and continues to do so, though we are not righteous in and of ourselves. As we stumble along, we grow as he does his work in us, though we will never be perfect. Jesus wants to teach us how to better love God and others. He wants our lives to produce the relational fruit described in Galatians 5:22–23. He transforms how we see the world, and what we value and consider important.

This second attribute of a disciple is primarily a *spiritual* response to the Holy Spirit. It speaks to people at the heart level, as they assimilate the Word of Christ and allow the Holy Spirit to transform their inner being (Eph. 3:14–18). Jesus is moving in their life and causing changes in their heart that lead to the development of their character. Far too many of us assume that discipleship is merely the transfer of information leading to behavior modification. But discipleship, at heart, involves transformation at the deepest levels of our understanding, affection, and will by the Holy Spirit, through the Word of God and in relationship with the people of God.

3. "Fishers of Men"

The final three words in this verse indicate a response of action, something that affects what we live for and do. If our acceptance of Jesus begins in the head and extends to the heart, it leads to a change in what we do with our *hands*.

In other words, a disciple of Jesus is saved for a purpose.

This means that we join Jesus on his mission to love and reach a lost and hurting world.

For their entire lives, Peter and Andrew had been fishers of fish. Fishing was all they knew. They would throw a net into the water, wait a while, and then haul out fish to sell at the market. Now Jesus was going to change all that. From now on they were going to fish for men. Jesus was giving them a new purpose—living out his purpose by helping in God's work to bring people to salvation in Jesus Christ.

Disciples of Jesus respond in a similar way today. When we spend time with Jesus, his Holy Spirit begins to work on us from the inside out. The passions and desires that used to drive us—love for possessions, fame, power, or prestige—just aren't as important anymore. Though those desires are still there, we have the Holy Spirit using the Word of God and the people of God to remind us about what really matters and the true destiny of the world. Now we are seeking his kingdom first, and we are beginning to see the world from Jesus' perspective. We begin to care about the things that God cares about, especially lost people.

Paul states it this way in 2 Corinthians 5:15–20 (ESV):

> He died for all, that those who live might no longer live for themselves but for him who for their sake died and was raised.
>
> From now on, therefore, we regard no one according to the flesh. Even though we once regarded Christ according to the flesh, we regard him thus no longer. Therefore, if anyone is in Christ, he is a new creation. The old has passed away; behold, the new has come. All this is from God, who through Christ reconciled us to himself and gave us the ministry of reconciliation; that is, in Christ God was reconciling the world to himself, not counting their trespasses against them, and entrusting to us the message of reconciliation. Therefore, we are ambassadors for Christ, God making his appeal through us. We implore you on behalf of Christ, be reconciled to God.

Being on a mission means that we acknowledge that we're saved for God's kingdom purposes. Our mission is not simply to come to church each Sunday, to be nice to other people, or to cram a lot of biblical facts inside our heads. It's not even to give money to the church so that the pastors can carry out the mission of Jesus. It's for every disciple to join in God's mission in this world, to participate with God's purposes in the world. The world is hurting and lost. People are dying and going to hell. We can give no greater gift of love than to share the good news that brings people into a relationship with God through Jesus. Inspired by Jesus (literally), we seek to love people and tell them what we have found in him.

With Christ's mission in mind, we understand that we were knitted together in our mother's womb by God for acts of service and ministry in his kingdom. We are all ministers of Christ and have

God-given abilities that can be used for God to glorify him. Our life experiences can be used by God; even our mistakes can be redeemed so that in our failure, we reveal God's mercy to lost people. Ephesians 2:10 tells us that we have important work to do which God had planned before time began.

As we see, the third attribute of a disciple—that we are "fishers of men"—is a commissioning, a call to action. It speaks to us at the hands level: we use our abilities and what God has placed in our hands to serve Jesus.

Putting all three attributes together, we see that a disciple is a person who

1. is following Christ (head);
2. is being changed by Christ (heart);
3. is committed to the mission of Christ (hands).

This is how we define a disciple. And this is what churches need to be seeking to make. Given the state of most churches in America today, this requires a shift: from simply making converts to reaching people and discipling them. Our goal is to present people as mature in Christ (Col. 1:28). When this is the goal, it changes everything.

STORIES OF EFFECTIVENESS

Richie Shaw is the lead pastor of Real Life Ministries in Spokane. We've asked him to describe some of the challenges he has faced as he and his team have worked through this process of creating a singular definition of discipleship and then living that out as a church. Real Life Ministries Spokane began in February 2010 with thirty people and three small groups. Today, as God is working in and through his people, the church has exploded numerically, and people are becoming spiritually mature.

Richie wrote,

> I had left pastoral ministry and was working as a landscaper back in Coeur d'Alene, Idaho, where my wife's family was from. I had become disillusioned and did not think I would ever want to play a part in a church again.

But I joined Jim Putman's small group, and there I began to hope again that Jesus' church could work. After some time, Jim brought me on staff. After I served for a couple of years as a home groups pastor, he then asked me to take another step and become a church planter in the neighboring city of Spokane. I didn't want to be a church planter at first, but after praying for some time with my wife, I responded to God's call in obedience. I was humbled that Jesus would want to build his church through me.

As we prepared a core team from people who lived in Spokane, we understood quickly that most of these thirty crazy people had not ever seen or tasted the biblical DNA of Jesus' church. How were we, this ragtag crew, going to become Jesus' church? Fears ruled most of us, paired with hurts from previous church experiences, and doubts of young leaders like me (thirty years old) ... This all seemed so impossible.

Long before we had a Sunday morning worship experience, we began setting definitions of real discipleship and relationship in place, based on Scripture, in our weekly small groups and in many a discussion over dinner or in a coffee shop. We took concepts from Scripture and put them into action in our lives. As soon as these bricks of the foundation were being set into place, the conflict began to arise. Some of us wanted to make the church more like what we had experienced before; some of us didn't want to make adjustments in our lives to align our lives with the gospel. These fights led us to crisis moments—for me as the leader, I needed to ask, Will I acquiesce to keep some of these people happy? Or will I learn to put real relationship to the test and call us all to an ideal place, to live out biblical discipleship in real relationship?

This was the most trying time of my leadership I had ever experienced. I had seen Jim lead, but it was different as the point man. I had never gone toe to toe with people, fighting for unity with Jesus' heart in our lives. I had talked conceptually about church for a decade. I had led groups before. I had preached sermons before. But I had never really had to lay it on the line for the sake of Jesus' message and model as the main leader.

I learned rapidly the need for trust in my relationship with God and in my relationships with my new teammates, as well as forgiveness (I open my mouth and make many messes). I believe RLM Spokane would and still could easily become another church in another city in another nation that goes through the motions of a good religious system without the life of the Spirit of God flowing through it. Our heart was to learn to be Jesus' church. We know that his presence and power is ultimately what changes human hearts, not my great system. So for us to give Jesus that opportunity to work in us and through us, we had to mortar the bricks of his DNA into place in our own hearts and lives, as well as in those of the next spiritual generation.

This first group grew and multiplied into three groups, which all branched to six groups within a matter of two months. Soon we were gathering monthly to vision cast what could be if we all learned to be Jesus' church together; we were connecting more people into these relational environments and starting new groups. As we started our twelfth group, we launched weekly gatherings with around two hundred people in attendance, and almost 80 percent of those in attendance connected into real relationship with others learning to be Jesus' church together.

This was eighteen months ago now. We have since seen Jesus continue to establish his DNA in our lives. If you were to cut one of us open, you would see the passion of Jesus spill out. Our passion is to pursue a real relationship with Jesus, where he speaks and we obey. A passion to be in real relationship with a real spiritual family, where real grace is needed and given. A passion to see the next spiritual generation raised up as an army. It is a passion to see Jesus' glory spread through this city and to the world. It is a passion to pursue people with the conviction that the greatest disciple maker has for each of us. A passion to develop people from where they currently are to help them become the men and women God is calling them to be. As we bleed this passion, this DNA into every life we come into contact with, we see Jesus growing his church.

We now have close to eight hundred people who call this their church, and over forty groups growing and multiplying in every area of this city. Over one hundred people have been baptized up to this point ... Lives continue to be transformed.

We are months away from starting a second location for gathering the church in another part of the city. We are blown away as people are connecting to Jesus in masses.

That's what we're talking about!

When a church has a commonly understood definition of discipleship, they have begun to make the first shift toward a renewed emphasis on discipling people. Once a person has met Christ and has taken the first step to follow him, they aren't left to wander alone. There is a solid, organic structure in place to help them move forward in spiritual maturity. Yes, there is a worship service that is vital to the church's life, and yes, there is organization, but it all leads to relational environments where people who have the same definitions live them out day to day. Believe me, that isn't easy. Many conflicts arise, as is normal with broken people who forget or who think they have communicated well, but haven't. However, when we fight for unity and alignment, something special happens.

So that's the first step: start with a common, biblical definition. Know where you want to go, and once your definitions are in place, you'll be ready to ask the next question: how do people begin to grow in their faith? Where do you start the process?

That's what we'll cover in the next chapter.

KEY POINTS

- A church must agree on the definition of its most important function, discipleship. Therefore, there must be agreement on behalf of all the church's leaders regarding this simple yet incredibly vital foundational question: what is a disciple?
- We draw our definition of discipleship from Matthew 4:19, where Jesus said, "Follow me, and I will make you fishers of men" (ESV). We apply this to mean that a true disciple of Jesus is a person who follows Jesus, is transformed by Jesus, and joins with Jesus on his mission.
- Your church's definition of discipleship may be different or taken from a different text. But whatever the definition is, it needs to be biblically based and clear—especially in the mind of every leader in your church.

Chapter 3

HOW TO START GROWING PEOPLE

If you want to make disciples, where do you start?

A couple of years ago, Jeremy Brown accepted the invitation to plant a church in Jackson, Tennessee. He is a Christlike guy with black glasses, a shaved head, and a sense of calm about him. But imagine for a moment the daunting task that he accepted. He moved to an unknown city and started a church from scratch with a small launch team. Their mission began with a quest to reach disconnected Christians and the lost and hurting in the community. It seemed like a hugely intimidating, ill-defined challenge: "See all those people? Go and make disciples out of them." In other words, it's your job to take these people and help them move from spiritual immaturity to spiritual maturity.

Where would Jeremy even start? What subjects should you cover to help your launch team to live out this mission? What programs do you create to support that mission? Let's get back to Jeremy after first considering an analogy.

Imagine that you are a medical doctor in charge of a number of residents at a large hospital. You are told to teach these med students the knowledge they need to be a doctor and to demonstrate appropriate expressions of empathy and compassion for suffering patients, and help them grasp the best methods and practices for restoring a patient to health. How do you accomplish this task? You break it into manageable pieces.

First, you begin by recognizing that an apprenticeship like this will take several years. You consider how to impart this knowledge a little at a time, with each successive year building on the last. As the residents mature and grow in their understanding, bedside manner, and abilities, more knowledge and responsibility is given to them. Their advancement in the program is about more than just their intelligence or grasp of the facts. It's about how they progress in the overall developmental *process*. Obviously, a third-year student should exhibit more maturity than one in the first-year, because that student has had more time to grow and develop in each key area of growth. Of course, you know that this is how it works in every school and even in every sports program, and honestly it works this way in Christianity as well.

The same is true for making disciples. And it was a process like this that Jeremy adopted as God led him to create a disciple-making church.

It might seem strange to categorize people into spiritual development levels. In the church, we are taught not to judge people, and categorizing people into groups might feel akin to judging them. But that's not what we are doing. Judging implies that we are issuing a final verdict on their character or morality. Instead of condemning them or placing them in a category that they can't move out of, we are seeking to assess their level of spiritual maturity in order to help them move forward and grow. An intentional leader understands the field of study he is attempting to teach. He is also able to evaluate where a student is on that journey and can create environments that will push their students to further knowledge and growth.

It can be very helpful to name the stages of growth for a disciple, understanding the basic characteristics and needs of each stage and recognizing some of the key phrases that people say in order to help you identify their current stage of growth. Jesus made it clear that you can know a tree by its fruit and that out of the overflow of the heart the mouth speaks. In other words, you can tell where a person is by understanding the stages of the journey they are on, as well as the things they might do and say. These things reveal where they are on the road to maturity. An accurate assessment helps you know where to begin as you develop a plan to help them move forward.

Remember, it's always about helping people to grow, never about hurting or hindering them.

A BIBLE-BASED PROCESS

This concept of spiritual assessment is entirely biblical. As we look at the twelve disciples, we observe that these were all men who went through a *process* of spiritual maturity. Remember that Jesus chose them to follow him, and while they did, he was making them into men who looked more and more like him as they spent time with him. It is both comforting and humbling to know that we are all in a process of spiritual growth and that no one fully arrives at the destination of perfection in this life. We grow by the grace of God and can slip in and out of various stages at different times in our lives. Every person can slip back into immaturity if they are not careful. That's why it is helpful to have a tool, and the skill to use it, that allows us to quickly and accurately assess where we are during any given time, as well as where the one we are discipling is. A good understanding of how to assess is helpful for many reasons. It can help leaders in the church know what to expect (and not to expect) from the people they serve and disciple. When you don't rightly assess someone, you can make the mistake of putting that person into a leadership position he or she cannot handle. You can end up placing someone in charge of important things even though that person does not have the maturity to be where they are, and this can really take the church down the wrong roads. Church leaders may look at the people in their congregation and assume certain things based on how long a person has been a Christian, how long that person has been attending church, or what titles or positions he or she holds or has held in the past. But these assumptions can miss the real story. They are not always an accurate reflection of where a person is at in the process of discipleship. Time in a church building does not have any bearing on a person's true state of maturity.

For instance, a pastor may look at a man named Ben, a forty-five-year-old member of his congregation who has been a Christian since age twelve. He has been successful in his career and is a capable leader in the secular business world. He has been attending the church for over thirty years, has been a Sunday school teacher, a youth sponsor, a deacon in charge of the van service, and he has just been asked to be an elder.

Great problems are likely to arise as Ben begins serving as an elder, however. He has never developed the habits of mature discipleship through daily Bible study and prayer. He has never been taught how to minister to others outside of the basic programs of the church. If you were to ask him to branch his home group into two groups so that new believers can be discipled, he might even grow angry and resent the intrusion into his group. After all, he and his wife "have made some great friends there," and they don't feel that it's right to ask them to move out of their comfort zone just so someone else can be included. He might say he has no leader capable to lead the other group, even after all of these years. You see, Ben may hold a position of leadership, but that doesn't *necessarily* mean he's spiritually mature enough to understand the mission of the church or to believe that investing in others for their good is an important goal. It doesn't mean that he and his wife have ever intentionally made a mature disciple in their own lives, and as you listen to them talk, it becomes very clear that though they have done much in the church, they haven't grown spiritually to the point of spiritual parenthood.

In just a moment, we'll look at five stages of spiritual growth and maturity. I want to emphasize that it's necessary not only to understand the levels but also to know what people's needs are at each level. Not even that is enough. An intentional disciple maker must also be able to create an environment in which those under his or her care are developed as believers. Again, the goal is not to simply categorize or label people; we want to help them grow! Some church leaders wrongly assume that all of the responsibility for discipleship and spiritual growth falls on them as the main vision caster and leader in the church. But this line of thinking will only frustrate them, exhaust them, and burn them out. Why? Because one person cannot do all that it takes to disciple everyone in the church (unless your church is the size of a small group). If he spreads himself out too thin, he will end up spiritually and physically unhealthy, and the people will not get the spiritual care and investment that it will take to help them grow to maturity as well. It will leave the congregation in a perpetual state of spiritual childhood. Because they are not taught, disciplined, and encouraged, they will end up demanding to be fed and cared for and never grow to the point that they can take care of others.

In reality, the responsibility for spiritual growth never rests on the disciple maker alone. We often tell people that there are three parts to the discipleship process. There is my part (the disciple maker), their part, and the Lord's part. I can't do their part, and I cannot do the Lord's part. I am responsible only for my part. Think of it this way. As I work as a leader to help move people toward spiritual maturity, it involves three parts:

My part: The things I can do to help a person in his or her spiritual journey.

Their part: These are the things that an individual is responsible for doing. If a person isn't interested in growing, there's really nothing I can do. The will must be engaged and responsive. There must be a desire and a hunger for change.

God's part: Ultimately, there are things that God alone is responsible for in helping people grow and develop spiritually. God is the one who transforms lives and brings about lasting life change. I need to understand my responsibility as a leader in light of God's role, learning to be patient and rest in God's plan and timing while being alert to opportunities he provides.

THE FIVE STAGES EXPLAINED[15]

The diagram "The Five Stages of Discipleship" illustrates the discipleship growth path we use at Real Life Ministries (and at the churches in the Relational Discipleship Network).[16] We recognize that although growth typically does not happen in a linear fashion, there is a path of progress, a direction we need to move in order to grow. The growth levels presented here are fairly simple and are drawn from Scripture, but there are some aspects that overlap with the spiritual growth continuum stages presented in the *Reveal* studies done by the Willow Creek Association.[17]

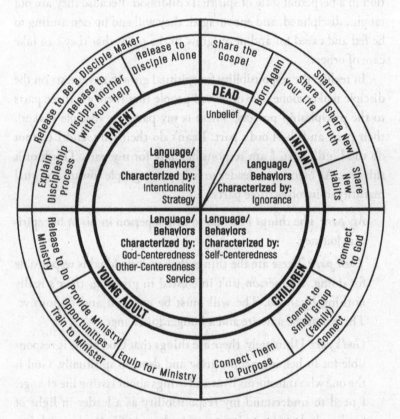

The Five Stages of Discipleship

Note that other than the first level of people who are spiritually dead, this is not a diagram that shows if a person has progressed to the point of being *saved*. When I say that a person is saved, I refer to the moment when we are made right with God through faith in Jesus Christ and spiritually born again. God gives us a new identity in Christ, and it is as saved disciples that we grow into our new identity. I emphasize this because it is no longer a matter of our justification; this is now part of our sanctification—the process of becoming what God has already declared us to be. Geiger, Kelley, and Nation describe it well: "As believers understand their identity, they are empowered by God to flesh out their identity in everyday life. Leaders who view discipleship through the lens of identity encourage and train people to live in response to the great identity God has given. Instead of beginning with behavior, leaders remind people of who they are in Christ. They connect the commands of God to the identity he secures for his followers, presenting obedience as the overflow of understanding and living the new nature Christ has given."[18]

We utilize a discipleship path with five primary stages of spiritual growth:

Level 1: Spiritually Dead

We begin at the top of the circle (in the twelve to one o'clock position). Ephesians 2:1–5 describes those who are "dead in [their] transgressions and sins." People in this stage have not yet accepted Christ as Lord and Savior. They may reject God, they may be seeking God, they may call themselves spiritual, they may even claim to know God or call themselves Christians, but there is no true fruit in their lives. They may claim to know Jesus, but they do not have the Holy Spirit living in them.

Not to be morbid, but have you ever seen a dead person, perhaps a body lying in a casket at a funeral? I realize this might sound like a strange question to ask, and I don't mean to offend anyone, but I ask it to make a point: what do you expect from a dead person?

The answer of course is, not very much. You expect them to decompose, and over time they will.

I ask this because I believe we need to set our expectations for *spiritually* dead people accordingly. As you interact with those who are spiritually dead to God, you may encounter some who exhibit unbelief or open rebellion. People may shake their fists at God or be angry at some hurt or injustice and blame God. There may be some level of spiritual interest—or none at all! My point is simply that we should not be surprised when spiritually dead people act this way. They are acting according to their dead human nature, and they cannot change until they have been made alive in Christ.

If you expect a dead person to be alive, you will be disappointed. Rather than be angry with the spiritually dead person for being dead, shouldn't we rather deal with the problem rather than their symptomatic behaviors?

We use the term "phrase from the stage" to help us identify where a person is at spiritually in their relationship with God. As I wrote earlier, Jesus made it clear that you can hear where a person is at the heart level when they speak (Luke 6:45). We teach everyone in our church this simple assessment tool as well. You can think of the "phrase from the stage" as a set of typical statements or questions that a spiritually dead person might say to you, such as:

- I don't believe there's a God.
- The Bible is just a bunch of myths.
- Religion is a crutch for the weak.
- Christians are just intolerant and homophobic people.
- There are many ways a person can get to God.
- I don't believe in hell. People just make their own hell.
- I've been a good person, so when I die, everything will be okay. I'll take my chances with the big man upstairs.
- There is no absolute right or wrong. If something's right for you, it might not be right for me, and vice versa.
- I'm spiritual, but I don't connect with any one religion.

Again, we teach our people to recognize these phrases so that they can know where a person is — not to judge them or condemn them but to help our people better know how to pray and respond, to understand what part Jesus wants to play in their lives right now. Just as a teacher will assess a student to better grasp where he or she needs help, a discipler can use these identifying phrases to assess a disciple (or potential disciple) to better understand where he or she needs help in their journey toward spiritual maturity in Christ.

The key concept is that a spiritually dead person does not have the life of Jesus within. This life is not there because they have no faith in Jesus as Savior and Lord. So what are the needs of people who are spiritually dead? First, they need love through honest friendships and relationships with believers. We often preach our best sermons with our lives and not our words. They need to be introduced to Jesus and to see the life of the gospel lived out. They need answers to their questions about the Bible, God, and Christianity. And they need a clear explanation of the gospel and an invitation to trust and follow Jesus. We refer to this as *pre-conversion* discipleship. It all needs to be done in an environment of love and prayer. The great news of Jesus is that if a person responds, he or she can be born again (John 3:3–5).

Level 2: Infant

Looking again at the diagram of spiritual stages, we see the next category in the two to three o'clock position on the wheel — the infant stage. First Peter 2:2–3 describes people who are like newborn babies, craving spiritual milk so they can grow in their salvation.[19] People at this stage are spiritually alive; they have made a decision to follow Jesus, but that's about as far as they've gotten! They can be brand-new believers, but this may also include longtime "Christians" who have remained stagnant in their faith.

The writer of Hebrews describes those he is writing to as people who are still living on milk when in fact they should be eating solid food for the mature and teaching others (Heb. 5:12–14). Spiritual infants tend to lack knowledge about what Jesus taught. They are not unintelligent; they are simply uninformed and in need of truth. Often they are the product of the culture they live in. The Holy Spirit is working in the infant, and there is receptivity to what the Word says. But they may have also gotten mixed up with the philosophy of the world, combining it with Scripture in a hybrid that works for them or at least at this point they think it is working for them. Their lives are generally all about them and what they think works to fulfill their perceived needs. Like actual infants, they don't know any better. They have been trained by the world to consume, so naturally they look to their pastor and the church as a service that will cater to their needs.

Consider what we typically expect from an infant. We know that babies are messy, loud, and need a lot of care. We expect them to need constant attention. We know it will take time for them to grow and mature. We know that there will be demands on our time, that it will require patience, that there will be mistakes along the way. But we also know that there are wonderful joys in raising kids. There is the excitement that comes with seeing a child grow up. Almost every step of growth is fresh and new, a cause for celebration. In fact, when a person first becomes a follower of Jesus, the contrast between their old life and their new life is sometimes so pronounced, it feels like a spiritual party.

When people are spiritual infants, the things they say will express the state of their heart. As you talk to a person in this stage, you may hear one or more of these phrases:

- I need to go to church regularly? I've never heard that before.
- I need to pray regularly and read the Bible regularly? I've never heard that before. How would I do that?
- I didn't know the Bible said that.
- Tithing? What's that?
- I've always connected with God through nature. Being outdoors is my church.
- I don't need anyone else. It's just me and Jesus.
- I need someone to regularly care for me.
- I know Jesus is God, but isn't karma real too?
- *Trinity?* Huh? Now you've got me confused.
- My wife and I just got baptized, and on the way home from church we got into a big fight. What's up with all that? I thought Jesus was supposed to take care of all our problems.

As you can tell, there are usually lots of questions. The key concept is that infants don't know much. They don't understand yet what it means to follow Jesus. They aren't aware of the ways in which they need to change.

So what are the needs of spiritual infants? They need someone to care for and feed them so they can grow and thrive. Eventually they will learn to feed themselves, but at this point, they don't really know how. They need the personal attention of a spiritual parent. They need protection and guidance during this vulnerable stage of discipleship. The devil often will try to get at them through those who would lead them astray—maybe a Mormon missionary at the door or even a so-called Christian program on cable that causes them to believe in promises that the Bible doesn't make. At this stage, they need the truths of the Christian faith taught and modeled for them. And they need to develop new habits that form new patterns for living as a follower of Christ.

Level 3: Child

The next stage of spiritual development is the child stage, found at the three to six o'clock position on the diagram. The apostle John often referred to the early Christians he pastored as his children (1 John 2:12).[20] And in 1 Thessalonians 2:10 – 12 the apostle Paul describes himself as a spiritual father who, in dealing with his children, must encourage, comfort, and urge them to live lives worthy of God. People in this stage are continuing to grow in their relationship with God, and they are beginning to grow in their relationships with other Christians as well. They have learned enough of the Christian "language" — the teachings of Jesus and the Scriptures — to be able to converse with other believers. They are beginning to apply God's Word in their lives and are walking with other growing disciples in their spiritual journey. Though they are growing, much of their spiritual life still revolves around them — meeting their needs, their desires, and their interests. As children, they are still quite self-centered, not yet fully oriented to the focus on others that marks people who are living in maturity in God's kingdom and family.

A spiritual child can be a relatively new Christian, or it can be a person who has been a Christian for many years. There are spiritually immature people who have attended church services for sixty years. And there are some spiritually mature disciples who have been Christians for just a few years. It's not the amount of time that passes that marks the difference between mature and immature; it's what has happened or not happened in a relational discipleship process during that time. How has he or she allowed the Holy Spirit to bring change and develop the likeness of Christ?

Think about the characteristics of a typical child. A child can do some things for himself. Yet they are still quite dependent on the care and guidance of his or her parents. A child can be active and joyful, as well as innocent and fun to be around. Yet they also are unaware that they are self-centered, focused on their own needs and without regard for others. As Romans 14 teaches us, a child can also be dogmatic, seeing the world in rigid, black-and-white terms, even concerning things that are not supposed to be black-and-white. A child can be overconfident, prideful, and full of himself, but they also can be insecure, timid, shy, and full of self-loathing or defeat. Spiritual children may have a connection to a church family, but their world still revolves around themselves. They may serve the church, but usually they serve because it is expected and usually only as long as the benefits outweigh the costs. Children crave affirmation and approval, and they will usually do the right things if they are rewarded in a way that pleases them.

As in the other stages, when someone is a spiritual child, their words reveal it. The key marker of this stage is being developmentally self-centered. The "phrase from the stage" for spiritual children often involves one or more of the following statements:

- I don't know if this church is meeting my needs anymore. Maybe I should go to a different church that does better.
- Don't branch my small group into two. We won't get to be with our friends.
- Who are all these new people coming into our church? The church is getting too big. It's too hard to get a parking spot anymore.
- Why do we have to learn new songs? I like the old hymns better.
- I didn't like the music today. They should play more contemporary stuff.
- No one ever says hi to me at church. No one ever calls me to see how I'm doing. No one spends time with me. The pastors don't care about me. Today in the lobby, a pastor looked right at me and didn't even say hello.
- My small group is not taking care of my needs like they should.
- I wasn't fed at all by that sermon today.
- Why don't they have a ministry to singles at this church? This church must not care about singles.

- No Christian should ever listen to hip-hop or rock. That kind of music is just unchristian.
- Well, I'd join the worship team, but no one's ever asked me.
- I was helping in children's ministry, but they didn't appreciate what I was doing, so I quit.

I am sure that even now you are remembering one of these statements being made to you by a Christian who had been in the church for years. Again, remember that the amount of time a person has spent in the church building does not determine their spiritual growth. So what are the needs of spiritual children? Their primary need is a strong relational connection to a mature believer so they can make the transition to a more God- and kingdom-focused life. They need someone who will help them learn how to make the developmental transition from dependency to learning how to spiritually feed themselves.

They need teaching about who they are in Christ, how to have close friendships with other believers, and what to expect (and not expect) from Christians. (Disappointment comes from unmet expectations, and there are no perfect Christians.) They need to learn to trust God in obedience, doing what the Word says rather than what their feelings tell them to do. As they grow, their lives will become more and more about God. They will learn to do the right things for the right reasons. And they will learn what it means to have a servant's heart, rather than one that is self-centered.

Level 4: Young Adult

Young adults are found at the six to nine o'clock position on the diagram. First John 2:13–14 describes people who are spiritually young adults. It says they have overcome the Evil One, and the Word of God abides in them.[21] Spiritual young adults are making a shift from being self-centered to being God- and other-centered. They are beginning to reorient their lives around God's Word and his people and mission. They are starting to understand that God has called them to give to the body of Christ, rather than simply take. They are involved in ministering to others, putting the needs of others first, and being doers of the Word — not just people who hear it and accumulate head knowledge. They have learned to do this for the right reasons—because of what Jesus has done for them. Even when people fail them, and they will, they do what they do because Jesus has never failed them.

As young adults in the faith, they want to serve God. They do it with the zeal, energy, and joy that the Spirit provides. They see the world as a place that needs changing. Spiritual young adults are beginning to see that God has created them for a purpose, and their priorities have started to change. They look for places to serve and may join the worship band, serve in the children's ministry, or occasionally speak or teach in front of larger groups of people. As they grow more secure in Christ, they tend to grow less judgmental and find it easier to overlook others' faults. They are excited about their involvement in the church, and even when they are not, they are learning to be faithful. They have begun maturing in their faith and are learning to focus on fitting their skills and passions to God's kingdom purposes.

As you speak with a spiritually young adult, you may hear one of these "phrase from the stage" statements:

- In my devotions, I came across something I have a question about.
- I really want to go to Uganda on a mission trip this summer. I know I'm ready for it. I know God has big plans for my life.
- I just love being a worship leader. I think it's something God has gifted me in, and I love to see an entire congregation lifting their hands in worship when I'm leading.
- I have three friends I've been witnessing to, and our small group would be too big for them, so can we branch so they can come?
- Brandon and Tiffany missed our group, so I called them to see if they're okay. Their kids have the flu, so maybe our group can make meals for them. I'll start.
- Look at how many are at church today—it's awesome! The closest parking spot I could find was two blocks away!

The key concept with spiritual adults is they are orienting their lives around God and his perspective. What are the needs of these spiritually young adults? First, they need a place where they can learn how to serve. They need a spiritual mentor who will coach and debrief them on their ministry experiences. They need deep, ongoing relationships with people who offer encouragement and accountability. They often need help to establish boundaries. They need guidance in responding to the expectations of people they serve. They need help identifying their gifts and receiving skills training. When they get hurt, and they will, they need to process the pain so they don't become disillusioned and cynical.

Level 5: Parent

The spiritual parent stage is found at the nine to twelve o'clock position on the diagram. Theologically, we believe that God is the one who births people spiritually. So strictly speaking, none of us are spiritual parents in this way. But this term is helpful in reminding us that those who grow and mature will usually do so under the guidance of spiritual parents; this is God's plan. We use the term "spiritual parent" rather than "spiritual adult" because we want to reinforce the concept of spiritual reproduction. In other words, when someone tells me they are spiritually mature, I ask them who they are discipling. If they tell me no one, then I am going to question whether they are spiritually mature. Spiritually mature people make disciples (have spiritual children, so to speak). If they are capable but are not parenting, then they are really just young adults at best. Parents, obviously, are responsible for raising children, helping them grow from infants to children to young adults, and then finally to be parents themselves.

Second Timothy 2:1–2 describes people who are strong in the grace that is in Christ Jesus. These are reliable disciples who have grown and matured to the point where they are now qualified to teach others.[22] A spiritual parent has a solid understanding of God's Word, a deep, abiding relationship with God, and a desire to be involved in raising up other disciples. Spiritual parents live out God's Word in their daily lives. They are kingdom-centered and God-dependent.

It's important to note that spiritual parents are not perfect. What marks a person, as a spiritual parent, is that they are intentional about building their own, ongoing relationship with Jesus, and as a result they are in relationships for the purpose of discipleship. They have learned to abide in Christ, and they are feeding themselves on God's Word so they have something to give to people they are parenting. Parents typically know how to determine where a person is in his or her spiritual journey, know where the person needs to go, and know how to get them there. As mature believers, parents understand that you never outgrow your need for a spiritual family, and they are humble enough to be involved in the church despite its many imperfections. When I say they are involved in the church, I mean they have relationships with believers in their lives, and they work with others in the organized body as a whole, using their God-given abilities. Parents are always still learning how to be parents, so they need help themselves as they make mistakes.

People who are involved in raising up others to join God's kingdom mission can be identified by one or several of the following "phrase from the stage" statements:

- I wonder if God is leading me to invest in Bill and help him mature in his faith.
- I want to help this guy at work. He asked me to explain the Bible to him. Pray for me as I spend time in the Word with him.
- We get to baptize someone from our small group tonight. When is the next foundations class? Getting him plugged into ministry is essential for his growth.
- Our small group is going on a mission trip. I am praying for God's wisdom as I give each person a different responsibility to help them grow.
- The most important discipleship is with my children. Will you hold me accountable to lead devotionals with my kids on a daily basis? I get so busy that I am not consistent with them.
- I want to be conscious of the influence of my words and actions when I go to the game with Bill and Betty. I easily get upset at the referees. As new Christians, Bill and Betty are hungry for guidance, and I want to set an example for them.
- I have a spiritual child in my small group who is causing conflicts;

pray that I will have patience as I lead them through this difficult stage.

- I have a young adult who is ready to be an apprentice in our group; it won't be long until we are ready to branch our small group.

The key concept for the spiritual parent is a mindfulness of the needs of the less mature disciples. What are the needs of spiritual parents? Most important, they need to have close peer relationships with other spiritual parents who are involved in making disciples for encouragement. Peer accountability and ongoing training help spiritual parents hone their skills. They also need assistance in learning how to delegate responsibility so that they take time to rest and avoid getting burned out. They need to be encouraged and freed to make disciples in the church. They need permission to develop people to maturity. So often our best disciple makers do not feel like they have a place in the church. They are not the main preacher, so they are reluctant to take a leadership role in the body. People who make disciples need to be celebrated and honored. I believe the adage that what you celebrate, people aspire to. If you celebrate only speakers and preachers, that is what people will want to become, or because they don't have that skill set, they will think they have no value. If you define discipleship and celebrate disciples making disciples, you will create a culture of discipleship.

Ask/Dr. Coleman

Some people have been Christians for many years yet are still spiritually immature. Why is this, and what can we do about it?

It's helpful for church leaders to identify the levels of maturity in the people they lead. One of the first realities to recognize in a church is that spiritual maturity and the number of years a person has been a Christian do not necessarily correspond.

Spiritual immaturity results from a lack of real discipleship. People may have been Christians for a long time, but they may not have been walking in the light all those years. They haven't been hungry and thirsty for righteousness. They haven't been with Spirit-filled people enough to see the challenge of moving forward and growing.

When I surrendered my life to the Lord in college, it was the presence of a godly student that convinced me there was more to being a Christian than I had found. His influence was a strong factor in my wanting to grow in the Lord.

The people of God are so important. If a person is around people who really love the Lord, it will rub off on them. People who aren't growing need to get around people who are growing, so they will see that there's something missing. They need to be challenged in a positive way and get excited to move toward spiritual growth.

Of course, just being with people is not the whole answer. Sometimes it's actually the problem, if you're with the wrong people. But when you're with someone who's a step ahead of you spiritually, then that is key.

A person needs to be only one step ahead of someone else to lead him. Many people are leading although they don't know a whole lot. But at least they know enough to do what they can to follow Christ. Hopefully, we have people who are far enough ahead that their life's example is a challenge itself for others to move forward and grow in grace.

What does spiritual maturity look like? It's what we imagine Christ would look like, if he were with us. Our imagination will exceed our comprehension, but at least it will give us a vision of what's before us. This is where the revelation of Christ in the Word is so vital. Because the picture we see of Christ in the Word is perfect. That picture is beyond our grasp, but we at least desire it.

Paul said to the Philippians, "I press on" to the mark in Christ Jesus. Yet he also stated, "Not that I have already obtained this or am already perfect" (Phil. 3:12–14 ESV). He was pressing toward it. There was something before him that he could envision.

That's why we are made: to know God and love him and find our joy in him. That's the reason why we exist. God will always be more than we grasp. But the more we discover, the more our hearts beat after that desire.

PUTTING IT ALL TOGETHER

As we close this chapter, I want to end with a word of caution. We need to remember that no stage of discipleship is more *important* than any other. Parents are not more valuable than children. Young adults are not more significant than people who are spiritually dead. All people are loved by God and welcomed into his kingdom. All are precious in his sight, created in his image. Readiness to be used in the mission varies, based on the person's developmental stage, but value does not.

The path of growth is described in a linear fashion to help you grasp the basic concept, but it is often cyclical. We often go back to earlier stages and find areas of our lives where we are uneducated or self-centered. Likewise, sometimes Christians at the infant or child stage can say and do things that display significant maturity or Christlikeness. People are complex; growth is multifaceted, even as it shows itself in traceable patterns. Mature believers can often slip back into immaturity if they are not careful. My wife and I got into an argument the other day, and I actually said to her, "You started it." Even as I said it, I realized what I had said. I didn't listen to the Holy Spirit for at least another hour as I defended myself, even in my own head. However, after a while, I had to surrender to what God was saying and ask for forgiveness. Spiritually mature people fail, but the longer and deeper the walk, the shorter the time period between the mistake and the repentance.

The existence of stages simply reminds us that inherent in our definition of discipleship is the understanding that disciples of Jesus grow and mature. We start with a commitment to trust and follow Jesus, and then, over time, we are changed by him. As Christ changes us, we become more mature. This maturity manifests itself as a growing desire to love and serve God and others and leads us to become spiritual parents who carry on Jesus' mission in the world.

How do we start on the road to spiritual maturity that eventually leads us to become disciple makers? Many of us were not taught that there was a process to go through after conversion. So we must now start to understand it and evaluate ourselves honestly. God can and will use other believers to help us do this. We always want to look at ourselves first. We then learn to identify the various levels of spiritual maturity in others, and work with them at each level, and then help each person transition to the next level. And so on.

To discover the specific place to begin, I need to tell you about the time I tried to teach my eight-month-old son to wrestle. (The results weren't good.) I'll tell you about that in the next chapter.

KEY POINTS

- Identifying what discipleship stage people are in can sound problematic. But what we're espousing is an overall beneficial step of the process. It's an assessment of spiritual maturity for the purpose of helping people move forward. Remember our goal is to present everyone mature in Christ Jesus (Col. 1:28). We want to create a movement of mature disciple makers who can make disciples.

- Church leaders will often falsely assume that all the responsibility for helping people mature spiritually falls on them. But that's not true, and this thinking will only frustrate, exhaust, and burn out leaders.

In reality, the responsibility rests on the shoulders of three people — the disciple maker, the person being discipled, and God.

- Effective spiritual assessment involves four components: (1) identifying the stages of growth for a disciple, (2) understanding the basic characteristics and needs of each stage, (3) recognizing key phrases that people say in each stage, and (4) helping the person develop and move forward.

- The five stages of spiritual growth are: (1) spiritually dead, (2) infant, (3) child, (4) young adult, (5) spiritual parent. If a person is saved, that person was saved for a purpose — the born again are given a new DNA that, when developed and becomes fully grown, will result in a mature disciple who makes disciples. It's every Christian's destination and destiny.

Chapter 4

THE FOUR SPHERES

In what areas does a disciple need to grow?

While training pastors and church leaders, I'm often asked a simple yet important question: "What does that actually look like?" In other words, in what *specific* ways does a disciple need to grow?

I'll typically answer by first asking the pastors and leaders in the group to share what they've done in the past or what's been hardest for them to put into practice in their churches. This is a difficult question for some leaders because they were never discipled themselves. They have never been exposed to an intentional process of discipleship and aren't sure what to focus on. Most have been exposed to a school-like system that builds on information accumulation, but again there is much more to disciple making than just head knowledge. Perhaps they initially learned about God in a Sunday school class or while attending a Bible college, but that first step of discipleship was a person imparting biblical information, with little life-on-life contact. Others have been taught that a mature disciple begins by grasping the right doctrine and then develops skills to teach others. Some leaders think they are relational, but when pressed on the point, they admit that they have few close friends in whom they confide. They do not have people they can confess sin to and receive help from, friends who will hold them accountable.

Since they have never been discipled themselves, these leaders find that they have a limited grasp on how to make disciples. They know the larger brushstrokes: popular concepts about how to do church that involve things like "teaching the Word" or "getting people into small groups" or "having relevant worship." But many leaders admit that these components, disconnected from relationship and an intentional process, are not enough. And these isolated components aren't producing the intended results where it counts—in real life. What they need is a clear, biblical model that intentionally leads people through the discipleship process.

MEET THE FOUR SPHERES

Many church leaders we work with come to the place that they understand that discipleship needs to be defined and that they need to create systems that allow for relationship. They also accept that mere understanding of the doctrine of salvation does not mean that a person is Christlike and mature in their faith. It often leads to the question, What specifically do we teach people in these relational environments? After studying the Scriptures, we identified what we call "the four spheres." This model is now the what in the midst of the how in our church. It outlines how a disciple grows in four main spheres of life:

1. In his relationship to God
2. In his relationship with God's family, the church
3. In his home life
4. In his relationship to the world

This means that in each sphere, a disciple understands God's commands and submits to his authority (head), is transformed by Jesus (heart), and joins Jesus on a kingdom mission (hands) in all of these areas of their lives. As a disciple abides in Christ, each sphere of his or her life is transformed. So many Christians, even pastors, have understood that they were to love other members of the family of God, but have neglected their own family. Many have said church is church and business is business, so the net result is that they are not true disciples of Jesus where they do business. So the very place that was meant to be the mission field for a believer was ignored and those who could have been won were turned off by the non-Christian behavior of one who might even be a leader in the church.

The four spheres also relate to the levels of growth we discussed in the previous chapter. Since people grow at different speeds, we should take care that we seek to disciple them in a way that is appropriate to their level of spiritual maturity. Again, it can be helpful to compare this process to a parent raising children. As my own children have grown, I have learned that I need to teach them what is fitting for the stage of life they are in. When my children were young, I tried many times to teach them things they were clearly not ready for. I still have a picture of my youngest son wearing a singlet (a wrestling uniform — kneepads, headgear, and all) when he was only eight months old. I had dressed him in the singlet because I'd heard somewhere that it was good for parents to read to their child even when the child was still in the womb. I applied that wisdom to my love for wrestling and figured that giving my son as much exposure as possible at a young age would be good for him; it would lead to a love for wrestling. The point is I had to set my expectations accordingly, resigning myself to the fact that he wasn't going to be a wrestling champ anytime soon.

Trying to teach an eight-month-old to wrestle is obviously a mistake, but over my years in pastoral ministry, I've made similar mistakes as I've tried to teach people how to be fully devoted followers of Christ. I've asked people to lead when they clearly weren't ready to lead. I've expected certain types of behaviors from people, even though their hearts weren't yet at the place where they wanted to act that way. I've grown upset when people haven't given me the response I was hoping for.

Over time, I've learned that there are seasons in a person's life when there is a strong desire to learn. Children, for example, want to be with their parents. A young boy will run to his father when he arrives home from work and beg his dad to drop everything to play with him. In this early stage, a child will listen and naturally seek to ingest whatever knowledge he can by listening and watching his father.

As that child grows older, he becomes a young adult. He will begin to think he knows everything, and if you are to teach him anything in this stage, you will need to pick your moments carefully and be alert to opportunities that arise. At this stage, a young adult wants to learn by doing things, and often he will listen to you only after he has tried and failed. It's important to mix affirmation with correction at this stage.

Eventually your children have their own families, and you will still get calls from time to time asking you for advice or saying thank you, because they finally understand just how hard it is to parent and raise kids. Do you see how this applies to the disciple-making process and the expectations we have for growth? Let me suggest that if you are discipling a spiritual child, you probably shouldn't expect him to thank you for your investment in his life—not yet, at least! Or if you are working with a spiritual young adult, she may be very idealistic and opinionated about her beliefs. That's to be expected from someone at her stage of maturity; they think they know everything and will have to learn that what they thought they knew doesn't always work. You need to remember that she may need to try and fail a few times to really grasp that her way doesn't work—just as you likely had to do when you were at that stage.

Having appropriate expectations for each stage takes some of the pressure off you. It releases you from unrealistic goals and misguided attempts at defining success. It frees you to focus on helping the person grow right where they're at, as you tune in to where they are spiritually. When you set your expectations in a way that matches the stage of growth, people can be genuine with you, sharing how they really feel and what they really want.

With this in mind, let's take a closer look at the four spheres to better understand what the discipleship process looks like in each sphere of life. We'll do this by unpacking what Paul says in his letter to the Ephesians.

Ask / Dr. Coleman

What does it mean to grow as a disciple of Jesus? Describe the process of spiritual growth in your own life. How did you progress on the continuum from spiritually dead to spiritual parent?

Following Jesus is evidenced by love and obedience. Faith is not a static thing. It's not simply an intellectual consent to a historical truth. Rather, faith finds expression in the way we live. Faith is a commitment to live by what we trust our lives to. We trust our lives to the person and work of Jesus Christ.

To be like Jesus — that must become our obsession. We must want more of him who is our life. To know Jesus is to know eternal life, a life that never ends. It becomes more and more a desire as we grow in grace and knowledge. The more we learn, the more we want to learn, and the more we see how much we need to learn.

The principle of walking in what light you have will lead you to more light. And anyone who seeks the Lord, if he's sincere, you bet that he'll find the Lord. Because God is faithful. That's the secret of growing in grace — you walk in the light as he gives the light. There's always more, and the blood of Jesus Christ cleanses from all sins. That's the beauty and simplicity of the gospel.

Years ago I thought I was pretty smart. But as I write these words at eighty-four, I realize how little I know. I am, however, convinced more than ever of the gospel. Thank God that it is simple enough for even a child to understand. It's powerful because we never exhaust the infinite dimensions of God's love and what he wants us to become, as we have seen revealed in the Son.

In my conversion, the big question was my vacillating between whether or not to do the will of God—to follow Jesus. I had grown up in the church and would have called myself a Christian, but I really didn't understand the way of salvation.

It wasn't until I began to learn more about the simplicity of the gospel, and my own lack of true faith, that I turned to Christ in repentance and faith. I was a student at Southwestern University when it all came to a head. One day a friend asked me what I was going to do after graduation. Flippantly I answered, "Oh, I don't know. I might be a lawyer, even a preacher." Isn't it interesting that sometimes you'll say something prophetic without realizing it? Well, someone hearing that response later invited me to speak at a church. I didn't know anything about preaching, but I found a good Bible text— Matthew 6:33—and got some illustrations in *Reader's Digest*.

It wasn't much of a sermon, to be sure, but it led to one or two more invitations to speak, and finally a request to preach at a youth revival in Temple, Texas. Not knowing anything about evangelistic preaching, I began to read some sermons by D. L. Moody and R. A. Torrey, among others, and came across words like *born again* and *conversion*. For some reason, I had missed those words and their meaning while growing up in the church.

So in preparing for the meeting, getting into some solid biblical preaching, I came under conviction and began to realize my own self-righteousness and need of a personal savior. When I knelt at the cross, in brokenness and humility, I turned my life over to Jesus. Though I didn't understand theology, I knew whom I believed and was persuaded that he would keep that which was committed to him (2 Tim. 1:12).

I wanted to tell everyone about Jesus, yet I had no training in evangelism. So I had to build the road as I walked on it. Often I have wondered where the next steps would take me.

One memorable time was in my first pastorate. Three little country churches made up my circuit, one of which, for all practical purposes, was dead. As someone put it, there wasn't enough excitement in that church to ruffle the fuzz on a gander's nose. A couple of church splits through the years had so depleted the congregation that only about two dozen people were still coming, mostly women and children. It was a pathetic situation. I would go out and visit and try to get people interested in God, but they would only talk about the problems in the church.

We surely needed a revival. So I announced that there would be a prayer meeting at the church every night for a week. Though the men dismissed the idea, thankfully a few women came to pray. The second week I started to preach. Though some people began to attend the meetings, there was no response to the invitation. Going into the third week, now physically exhausted, I had a strange leading to do something I had never done before, nor expect to ever do again. Somewhere I had read that in the olden days it was a custom to ring the church bell when there was urgent news for the community to hear, like a notice of a funeral. Then I told the congregation that tonight I was ringing the bell for them—to seek the Lord while he may be found. There was no desire to draw attention to myself; I was heartbroken for my people, and I didn't know what to do.

Well, I rang the bell. Its tolling could be heard for miles through the still night. Soon some youth began to join me, and we continued to ring that bell for three hours until the sheriff came. Three of my church members had gone to the courthouse and pressed charges against me for disturbing the peace.

I met the sheriff at the door. His deputy with him was holding handcuffs in his hand. "People say they can't sleep with all this noise," said the sheriff.

"Sir," I said, "some of them need to be woken up. They're lost."

The sheriff looked me in the eye very intently, and then spoke with a more subdued voice. "Preacher, I've never been on a call like this before. But I'll tell you what—if you will just quit ringing that bell, I'll forget the whole thing."

Well, some of those old sinners did wake up. The church was full the next night. Revival broke out, and by the end of the week many people got right with God. I baptized twenty-five on Sunday.

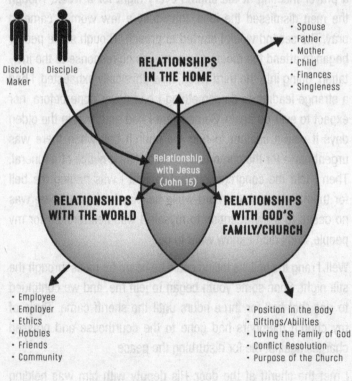

Disciple Maker Disciple

RELATIONSHIPS IN THE HOME
- Spouse
- Father
- Mother
- Child
- Finances
- Singleness

Relationship with Jesus (John 15)

RELATIONSHIPS WITH THE WORLD

RELATIONSHIPS WITH GOD'S FAMILY/CHURCH

- Employee
- Employer
- Ethics
- Hobbies
- Friends
- Community

- Position in the Body
- Giftings/Abilities
- Loving the Family of God
- Conflict Resolution
- Purpose of the Church

The Four Spheres of Life

Sphere 1: The Centrality of a Relationship with God

As a leadership team, we didn't just pull the four spheres out of our own minds or experience. We believe that Paul is a great example of discipleship and that he reveals his thoughts on the matter in the book of Ephesians. In the first two chapters of Ephesians, Paul sets the tone of his letter by reminding us that we are adopted as spiritual children of our heavenly Father because of the gospel. Paul reminds us that we are not accidents; our lives were planned before time began. He reminds us that we came to be born again spiritually, even though we were dead in our sin. He proclaims that we are saved by grace through faith, to do good works that God predestined for us to do before time began (Eph. 2:8 – 10).

Here we see the central importance of the first sphere: our relationship with God. This sphere is the core, the hub that unites the other spheres together. If we forget that we are saved by grace, that our security and our strength are from God and not from ourselves, then we fall into a form of salvation by works. Without the gospel, we will become proud because we will naturally compare ourselves with others, forgetting what *our* righteousness looks like to God (not good). More likely, we will become burdened with guilt and simply give up on wanting to grow to become like Christ. John 15 tells us that we must abide in Christ if we wish to bear fruit; it's a clear indication that our most important sphere is our personal relationship with Jesus. As branches connected to the Vine, we receive direction from Jesus through his Word, strength from his Spirit, and help from his people.

In the context of discipling someone, there are three questions you need to ask in relationship to this sphere:

1. *Head:* Does the person I am discipling know what Jesus teaches about growing in relationship to him? Is he or she willing to surrender to Christ? Is he or she spending time with Jesus so that they have the strength and direction to be who they are meant to be?

2. *Heart:* Are there visible changes happening in this person's life? Are they doing the right things for the right reasons? Have there been changes in their character? Are they showing

a consistent pattern of growing in love for God and for others? Are there signs that they are doing all this in their own strength, or are they humbly trusting Christ for salvation and abiding in him?

3. *Hands:* Are they willing to follow Christ in the direction he is leading them? Are they putting into practice what they are learning and wanting to do, what their head and heart are calling them to do? In other words, are they concerned about the salvation of others and are they using their gifts to help reconcile others to Jesus? Do they have the skills they need to do this?

Sphere 2: Relationships within the Family of God, the Church

As we read further in Ephesians, we see that in chapter 4 Paul shifts his focus from the central importance of our personal relationship with Christ and begins to discuss the effect that a relationship with Christ should have in our relationships with other believers. Paul widens his message to talk about how God's children relate to one another in God's family, the church.

The second sphere of relationships is where we grow as the body of Christ. Scripture tells us that when we are born again, we become part of the family of God and have a spiritual Father as well as brothers and sisters in Christ. It can be easy for us to accept the good news that we have a Father who loves us, yet fail to relate to other believers as brothers and sisters, but the two are connected.

As a family, the church works together and lives together in a network of loving relationships. In the days of the early church, many believers were coming out of a broken world and did not have family relationships in which they were encouraged, challenged, and loved. Some had seen their families fall apart, while others had lost their families because they decided to follow Jesus. The church is God's answer to these needs—a family led by shepherd-pastors who spiritually father growing disciples. In his own life, Paul modeled just such a relationship with his young protégé, Timothy.

If the first sphere of relationship is our relationship with Jesus, it should naturally lead us to living with and loving others in the second sphere, our relationships within the family of God. Paul, writing to the church, reminds us that we are committed to one other. We should build each other up and sacrifice our wants and desires for the good of the mission, to help other believers in need. In his letter, Paul gives instruction on how to deal with conflict and anger and on how to use the gifts God has given us to serve others. Again and again throughout Paul's letter to the Ephesians, we see the clear connection between a growing relationship with God and a growing relationship with other believers. As we walk with God, we learn to love our brothers and sisters in Christ.

Again, we should ask the necessary head, heart, and hands questions that relate to this sphere.

1. *Head:* Does the person I am discipling know what the Bible teaches about the church and the importance of his or her relationships with other believers?
2. *Heart:* Are they growing in their love for others in the body of Christ?
3. *Hands:* Have they developed the relational skills they need in order to have healthy relationships with other believers? Are they using their gifts to minister to believers who are in need, or are they doubting and in need of encouragement? Is there a skill that I should teach them to help them grow in this sphere?

Sphere 3: Relationships at Home

A third sphere of relationships that Paul addresses, in Ephesians 5 and 6, is the family. Paul discusses what the home should look like for a believer, how a husband should lead his wife and love her, and how a wife should respect her husband. He writes about the responsibility that mothers and fathers have to raise children in the Lord and about how children should act toward their parents.

This sphere is important for us to address, because it is possible for people to grasp the concepts of the gospel but fail to apply them in the home. As a disciple maker, Paul wasn't just interested in talking about an individual's personal relationship with God and about the relationships among believers in the church; he moved right into the home and gave clear instructions in this area. He understood that we cannot compartmentalize our relationships, that the Holy Spirit wants to influence every sphere of a believer's life, and that the best place to make disciples is in our own families. Not every Christian has the gift of leadership, but every believer is supposed to make disciples, and the most important place to focus is in our homes. I have always been convicted that it would be my biggest failure to win the whole world and lose my own children.

Many of the believers Paul was writing to had come to faith as an entire family but had not been taught how to be a Christian family. They didn't understand how to relate to one another in the way God had designed the family to relate. As believers walked with Jesus, Paul knew, they would need to exchange the world's understanding of self-centered love—what had been passed down to them from their parents and culture—and learn what it meant to love in the way of Jesus. Paul knew that the Holy Spirit would empower them and give them direction through the Word, and he knew that it would be necessary to have models of godly family life in the church, examples that people could look to and follow.

Sphere 4: Relationships with the World

Finally, as Paul moves through Ephesians 6, he addresses a final sphere of relationships, what we might refer to as the world. Paul speaks of what it means to be a slave and a slaveholder. Some say that 90 percent of the Roman world in Paul's time would have been considered a slave. We often think of slaves in the context of American history, and indeed there was some of that kind of slavery in the Roman world, but to be a slave could have meant that you worked for someone who paid your living expenses. That sounds more like what we deal with today. Paul was not endorsing slavery; he was just acknowledging the fact of slavery and explaining how a believer should act in the world they lived in. Today we can apply this to the context of our workplaces, in the relationship between an employee and his employer. Paul is speaking here of how believers are to act as they live in the world. Remember that back then, a person's world consisted of faith, family, and work. They did not have the time to be in little kids' soccer or, better yet, wrestling (my favorite). In our culture, we don't have to walk five miles for water or dig holes for a toilet. We have microwaves, and cars to get us places quickly. When I speak of the spiritual life in the world, I believe the principles apply wherever you interact with unbelievers. Paul makes it clear that believers are to work so that they can take care of their families as well as have something to share with other believers.

Paul makes it clear that when we are in the world, we represent Christ, and in what we do, we do not simply work for other people; we work for the Lord. In this sense, our work affects God's reputation. We work and live in a way that meets our physical needs, certainly, but at the same time we work in such a way that we serve as missionaries to a lost and dying world. Paul wants us to understand that our relationship with Jesus necessarily affects how we live and work in the world. Paul gives specifics in this area as well: people are to work hard, not be lazy, and be sincere and gracious even to people who aren't that way in return. He teaches disciples to be ethical and consistent and to live in such a way that even if someone does accuse them of doing wrong, the unbelievers will see their good deeds and glorify God.

PUTTING IT ALL TOGETHER

So let's put all of this together. Let's say that as a disciple maker, you are in relationship with a spiritual child. Where do you begin? In what areas does this disciple need to grow? Thinking through the four spheres can be a helpful way of coming up with a plan. Begin with the center sphere. The first area to focus on is helping this person learn to walk with Jesus. This can be as simple as committing to seek the Lord together. As you are praying and confessing sin and reading the Scriptures with this person, make sure you are explaining what you are doing and why. As you seek God's will for your own life, take time to explain how you come to know what God's will is, by sharing Scripture with the person. Encourage him to seek God's will for his life through Scripture the way you do. In this relationship, make sure you are being transparent and humble, sharing when you fail.

For the next step in the process, you might say something like, "As we seek to understand the truth of the gospel and who we are in Christ, let's start to look at the other three spheres of your life (mine too) and ask the question, What would Jesus have me do in my family or in the church?" You may have the person ask one of the following questions:

- Do I need to resolve a conflict or encourage someone?
- Do I need to serve somewhere or be more faithful in my involvement in the church?
- Do I need to take the initiative to lead my family to relationship with Jesus?
- Do I need to become a better servant to my wife (or husband) or find a way to connect in relationship with my son or daughter in a way that is more meaningful to them so I can earn the right to hear what is really going on in their life?
- Do I need to work harder when I'm at my job, or do I need to stop gossiping about my boss or stop listening to the jokes my coworkers tell?

Remember that you always come back to the center sphere, that a person's relationship with Christ can't be separated from any of the other spheres of life. This means that if something is wrong in one of the other spheres, it's usually a core issue that needs to be addressed first.

THE NATURE OF SPIRITUAL WARFARE

It can be helpful to notice how Paul closes his letter to the Ephesians. After discussing what it means to be a growing disciple in the various relational spheres, he gives a warning and an encouragement. We must never forget that the disciple-making process happens in the storm of spiritual warfare. Making disciples is not something we do in safe, neutral territory. There is always a battle to fight. As we help others deal with their sin nature and besetting sin, the devil will work against us and seek to frustrate the process and sideline people who are growing. Satan does not like to lose what he once owned.

But the good news is that we do not fight unarmed or unprotected. Paul tells the Ephesians that they need to put on the armor that God has provided for them.

In your own life, you too will struggle against the devil as you grow and change. This battle is ever present, and the enemy will try to persuade you to justify your own sin ... or he will shame you with it so you feel like giving up!

To succeed, we must be ready. We need to have our armor on, prepared to stand our ground.

BENEFITS OF USING THE FOUR SPHERES

Far too often I've heard of churches that share the gospel with someone, pray with them, and perhaps even baptize them, only to give them a Bible and tell them to come back to church next week. Few people survive past these initial steps, spiritually, and if they do, they often stay in an immature state for their entire life, never experiencing all that Jesus has for them.

When people become followers of Christ, it's important that we explain *how* they've entered into a lifelong relationship with him. I find it beneficial to explain the discipleship process to them early on, as well as the stages of spiritual development they will go through. Of course they don't fully grasp the idea that this will be a journey, nor do they understand the specifics of each step along the way. But at the very least, they understand that change isn't instantaneous, that following Christ is a journey we take together, and that they need help from others to grow up in Christ.

I often introduce the four spheres to them as well, telling them that being a Christian means that all of these areas need to come under Christ's control. I point out that it's in our best interest if they are under his control, as we tend to make a mess out of all we try to be lord over. I want them to understand that I am here to go through this journey with them and that they will always need to do life with someone; we don't graduate from relationships. I share with them that I need their help too and that we will do this together. I explain that my goal is to help lead them to a relationship with Jesus, and that only in Christ do we have the power we need to conquer sin. My job as a disciple maker is to help them focus on the most important sphere—their relationship with Jesus. If I start to work on the other spheres without giving them a firm grasp of what it means to be in relationship with Christ, meaning to help them to be secure in their identity in him, they will inevitably burn out and grow discouraged.

In all of this, we want to give people a *biblical* worldview. We do this by helping people see that the Bible is God's Word to us, how God speaks to us in every area of our lives. Disciples of Jesus want to know what Jesus wants. His Word is a light for our path, so when we read the Bible, we are constantly asking the questions, What is Jesus saying? And will I rely on his strength as he leads me this way?

STORIES OF EFFECTIVENESS

I close with a story about a woman named Traci who attends our church. Recently Traci found herself in a situation in which she had to use the four spheres in specific ways as she was interacting with her fellow employees in the workplace. Traci had just become a Christian, and in her small group she had learned what a relationship with Jesus was like. She understood that Jesus wanted to be Lord of every part of her life and that this meant not only her relationships with her family and in the church but her relationships at work as well.

Traci works as a psychosocial rehabilitator, and her supervisor at work had asked her to find a way of helping their clients gain skills and confidence by spending time socializing with others in a safe environment. Traci had been kicking around the idea of starting a craft group. The organization Traci works for operates under a contract with the state, so all of the groups she had done in the past had been nonreligious in nature. A craft group seemed like a good, safe idea.

Then, during one of our weekend services, Traci began praying in response to a question one of the pastors had asked, and she sensed that God was speaking to her. Immediately she knew the steps of obedience she had to take. She felt God nudging her, telling her that instead of a craft group, she should start a Bible study at work. Traci felt confident that this was the direction God was pointing her to follow, but she was still hesitant, not only unsure if she could do it but also wondering whether it would be allowed.

The following week, Traci sat down and shared her idea with her supervisor. She figured that if God wanted it to happen, he would make it happen. Surprisingly, the supervisor liked the idea, but she told Traci that she would need to take it to the management team for a decision. After several weeks, Traci had heard nothing back from her supervisor, and she assumed that her request had been denied. Then, to her amazement, she received a phone call granting her permission to start the group the following week. She decided that the first topic they would cover would be prayer, and afterward they would address topics like fear, anxiety, joy, and contentment.

That first meeting saw only two people attend. But after several more weeks, the group began to grow. Currently it's one of the highest-attended classes offered by that organization.

What did Traci learn from all of this? She learned to rely on God, to not be afraid to share her faith in God with others. She learned that God can work even in nonreligious settings, and that if you don't ask, then the answer is always no. Though her work environment is secular, her coworkers now know where she stands, and agency clients are growing in their abilities to cope with life's circumstances as they learn to rely on Christ. When Traci eventually asked her supervisor why the Bible study had been approved, she was told that the management team agreed to it because they trusted her and knew she would do it well. In other words, they saw the quality of her character as a growing follower of Christ. Because she had allowed Jesus to change the way she saw her work and the people there, she had become a wonderful example to others. That's what discipleship is really all about. As Traci grew in her commitment to Christ, it affected everything she did — including her work.

In the next chapter, we will look at the second shift in the process of transforming a church into a community that makes disciples. It's a shift from *informing* people to *equipping* them. I want to caution you that this next section of the book may be one of the most challenging parts of the shifting process for you.

Why?

It's where you will be asked to take a good, hard look at one of the key components of the shifting process, something so strategic that I'll give you this warning: if this part of the process doesn't see a shift, there's little else that can be done.

I'm talking about the man in the mirror.

That's right.

It's time to take a good, hard look at *yourself.*

KEY POINTS

- A disciple grows in four main spheres of life: (1) his relationship to God, (2) his interaction with God's family, the church, (3) his home life, and (4) his relationship to the world.
- The key that produces significant growth is not simply that a disciple is educated in each sphere; it's that a disciple follows Jesus in a holistic way in each of the four spheres. This means that a disciple understands God's commands and submits to his authority, is transformed by Jesus, and joins Jesus on a mission, in each sphere.
- People grow at different speeds, depending on their level of spiritual maturity, and we should expect this as church leaders. Don't expect a child to act like an adult, and don't allow an adult to act like a child without loving accountability.
- Spiritual warfare is always a part of the discipleship process, and Christians need to expect to contend with a battle in the spiritual realms, according to Ephesians 6.

SHIFT 2

From Informing to Equipping

Chapter 5

THE ROLE OF THE LEADER

What's the role of the leader in the disciple-making process?

When I first felt God's call to become a pastor, I entered pastoral ministry reluctantly because I didn't want to be the traditional pastor. I looked around at all the pastors I saw, and I thought, *There's no way I would ever want to be like that. Those guys might seem to have it all together, but that's not real. No one has it all together—especially not me.*

You see, I had struggled with substance addictions in the past and had seen the healing and restoration that can come through organizations like Alcoholics Anonymous. I'd seen the power of people being honest, sharing their struggles with one another and talking about their need for God. I had seen the power that comes when you have a sponsor (a disciple maker) in your life, and I had also seen what could happen when you try to figure things out alone. I thought, *That's the type of pastor I can be—one who is open and transparent about his own shortcomings.*

So that's how I chose to enter pastoral ministry. Flawed, real, broken, and genuine. I thought, *I can try to be perfect and polished, but that's never going to happen. Or I can enter ministry with authenticity—forgiven by God, continually cleansed from sin, and a model of growth, not perfection.* By God's grace, that's the type of pastor I'm still seeking to be today.

It continually astounds me how many pastors haven't discovered the freedom that comes from being transparent about who they are as a sinner saved by grace. I've talked with too many pastors who have lost their joy for ministry because of self-imposed pressure to be someone they are not. The stresses of the job have overwhelmed them, and they have become spiritual robots, on the verge of burn-out. Exhausted, friendless, and lonely, these men are prime targets for the enemy. Some are a step away from moral failure, others from quitting the ministry or putting themselves in cruise control and just collecting their paycheck. Others are more resigned — buckling down and holding the course until retirement.

This is not what the church needs. It's not what we want. Church leaders want to experience joy in what they do and have real relationships that sustain them. They want to use the right resources and do the right things and aim for the right goal. They want churches that produce lasting disciples of Jesus Christ — people whose lives are changed in lasting ways for the glory of God, people who live with spiritual maturity for the rest of their lives, people who fulfill the Great Commission and work to produce other disciples.

So how can we ensure that this happens?

The solution involves a fundamental shift in our thinking — from *informing* people to *equipping* them. You may think, *That's what I'm doing already. I don't want to give people more information; I want to see transformation!* But take an honest look. Is that really the focus of your ministry? I want to suggest that there are two issues involved in this shift. The first has to do with a leader's personal life, and the second has to do with his professional life. The first issue relates to who he is, and the second issue relates to what he does. Both are integral in the overall task of running a church, because a pastor or church planter sets the tone for what spiritual maturity looks like in a congregation. The pastor is the DNA of the church. We'll look more at the first issue (character) now, and then address the second issue (tasks) in the following chapter.

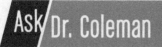

Ask Dr. Coleman

Describe one person who's been a spiritual mentor to you.

There have been many along the way.

What made it difficult at first is that I was never around any organizations, such as Campus Crusade or the Navigators, that were consciously seeking to disciple people.

Yet there were people who encouraged me along the way, even before I came to a point of conversion.

One was a Sunday school teacher I had as a high school student. She was an inspiration. I didn't understand the plan of salvation. But I have a plaque on my desk today that was given to me by Mrs. Anderson, my teacher. It simply says, "Prayer changes things." Absolutely, I'd say she encouraged me to take one step forward with God, even though I was still away from him.

I remember my dear mother. She was an inspiration to me, and I'd go to church with her. Unfortunately, my mind wasn't tuned in to what was going on. But Mom was consistent in her sweetness and love. I never heard her say an unkind word. Dad, though a believer, was more distant from the church, but his example of righteousness and integrity made a lasting impression on me.

After I became a Christian and as I began to grow, I searched out people who could challenge me in my faith.

When I came to seminary, I heard some boys praying up in the attic about eleven o'clock at night. So I joined myself to that meeting every week. One of those boys was an ex-GI. He was so serious about God, he'd bring you under conviction just to look at him. He went over to Borneo after graduation and spent more than fifty years there as a missionary before he died. Without his realizing it, he was a mentor to me.

When I was beginning to teach at the university level, I experienced the providence of meeting Billy Graham, and a friendship developed that has encouraged and inspired me to this day. The witness of many other godly men and women who have crossed my trail over the years has also made its mark on me.

Even now, at age eighty-four, I meet with a group of older men most Tuesday nights. Usually four or five of us meet together to encourage each other in the faith. One man is in a wheelchair, a dear man of God. He's been an influence on my life across the years. I don't know if I've made an important decision without talking to him about it. We never get beyond our need for spiritual encouragement, fellowship, and mentoring.

During most of the year, I meet with a group of young men, a practice I started nearly fifty years ago when I began to teach at seminary. We meet usually at six a.m., when things are still quiet on campus.

THE CHALLENGE OF AUTHENTICITY

On a recent trip to Israel, I interacted with a number of pastors in a discipleship consulting role. The hardest part of our time together was getting them to understand that they didn't need to look like they had it together all the time. They were used to being the answer men, the guys who knew everything and always had life under control. If you were to peek under the hood of their church, you'd find that these men were not really reproducing disciples as much as gathering people together. The little reproduction that was happening was unhealthy because the people who followed them thought they had to have it all together too.

They were producing groups in which no one talked, and whenever a person did have a problem, he stopped showing up at the meetings until they got things figured out and could fit back in with the "perfect people." Why? Because if a person was struggling or having trouble, then he felt like a failure. No one wanted to attend a meeting where they left feeling worse about their problems. So these churches had developed a system in which people most in need of the prayers and encouragement of others wouldn't come to the groups intended to help them. The leaders had *unintentionally* taught through their own model that it's not okay to share your struggles and brokenness with other believers. The lack of honest sharing from the leaders, the absence of vulnerability, had created a culture of perfectionism.

Working with these leaders, I reminded them that a leader is not simply a person who shepherds others; he also creates a shepherding *environment*. To create an environment like this, a leader must allow others to shepherd him as well. And that requires vulnerability.

I know this shift can be difficult for leaders. I'd been a pastor for many years when my son, as a young adult, made some devastating decisions with drugs and alcohol, decisions that led him to several near-death experiences and jail time. I had always been open about my failings, and so I was able to live in a safe environment, yet this was a whole new level of embarrassment and failure. During that time, I really could understand how many pastors feel about hiding or pretending or even quitting. The enemy immediately sought to shame me and I was tempted to keep all of this hidden, to not share it with anyone at our church. I felt ashamed and worried that people would criticize me or judge me for not leading my family well. We had raised our son according to scriptural wisdom, but he wasn't following what we had taught him. And I was frustrated with God. In my mind, he wasn't living up to his end of the bargain. The enemy told me that I couldn't share that, that I would lose my credibility if I were struggling at that depth of my soul. On a more pragmatic level, the enemy whispered that I might lose my job. The temptation to keep quiet about everything was strong—after all, a pastor is supposed to have his life and household all in order, isn't he?

Instead of hiding, I chose to go the other route. I went to the elders and staff of our church and told them what was happening. During that season, every day was filled with confusion, frustration, and pain for my wife and me, and the church leadership and staff helped us carry that burden. I shared what was happening with my home group as well, that our son was doing drugs and was completely out of control. I confessed that Lori and I were really struggling in our marriage under the pressure. We just couldn't get on the same page about how to handle this situation. I remember one night coming to the small group I was supposed to lead and saying, "Guys, I have nothing to offer tonight, because I'm just dying inside." Our friends gave us time to share, asking questions, listening to us, and praying for Lori and me.

The support of our church family was vital to my wife and me as we navigated that season of our lives. At one point, my son needed to stay in a rehab center, and it was going to cost us fifty thousand dollars. We didn't have the money and had no idea how we were going to pay for it. Unbeknown to us, our small group worked together behind the scenes and pooled their money to help us. They didn't have a lot of money to begin with, and what they gave didn't pay much of the bill, but it was still a meaningful sign of their care for our family.

After our son entered the rehab center, it was very important for him not to leave. At that time, I needed to be out of town leading a mission trip and would not have access to phones or email. Before I left, my wife and I agreed that we would not go get him, no matter what, if he did not complete the program. During this trip, our son was kicked out of the center. He had nowhere to go and ended up staying in a homeless shelter. (He had to stay there for four months.) Lori could not talk to me about what was happening, and she was struggling with the need to let him hit bottom. She texted our small group members and asked for help. All of the women came over to the house and just sat with her. She told them, "Here, take my keys. Because if you don't, I'm going to go get him." Again, it was a powerful time for us to be vulnerable, sharing our pain and struggle, and we were blessed by friends in our church family who walked through that experience with us.

The happy ending to this story is that my son, Christian, has now been sober for almost two years and is doing well today. Not only has he experienced freedom; he is now in ministry, and he and I have shared the story of that season of our life publicly with our entire church family.

All of this shows the power of honest vulnerability. If I had decided to rely on myself, keeping all of this hidden and not letting others help, I likely would have broken apart, burned out, or lost my family during that difficult season. Instead I chose to model the way of vulnerability, asking others for help and prayers. My dependency on them showed them that it's okay for leaders to fail, to have needs, to not have it all together. In doing my job, I was not just *informing* people about how to be Christians; I was *equipping* them to be ministers. In this case, I happened to be the one they were being equipped to minister to. God used that experience in my life to show others in our church that honesty and grace can change things. It helped set a culture that has affected our small groups. People are confessing their sins to one another and being healed of spiritual sicknesses that, in many cases, have held them captive for years.

A PASTOR'S LIFE AND CHARACTER

Let's consider two primary sections of Scripture that address the character of a leader: 1 Timothy 3 and Titus 1. Both of these passages list several qualities for godly leaders in the church: they are to be above reproach, self-controlled, respectable, the husband of one wife, not given to drunkenness and the like. This list of qualities reflects the character of the man, not his skill level or intelligence. Why is this significant? Because when the challenges and stresses of life become overwhelming, a pastor's behavior will flow from his character. How he acts — both privately and professionally — will spring from who he is.

Granted, there is some tension here. Some look at these descriptions of a church leader's character and feel that they just don't measure up. Many actually believe that to struggle in any way means you are not qualified. They read these lists and feel that they cannot share their struggles and faults with the church. They fear being fired or dismissed if they reveal any struggle with sin or evidence of spiritual weakness. They buy into the lie that a pastor needs to be a model of sinless perfection, and if he has struggles, they are somehow different from those of the rest of the people in the church. But the unintended consequence of leaders who buy into this mindset is a church culture in which the members themselves begin to feel a sense of unworthiness. People don't serve, volunteer, or lead because the false model they have been given doesn't seem to have sin issues or struggles. Nonbelievers know that no one is perfect and assume that the church is filled with hypocritical leaders who cannot be honest and real. They want nothing to do with the church and are turned off by the lack of transparency. Churches like this do not model the reality of the Christian life. They do not model repentance, grace, and faithfulness. And this is one of the greatest hindrances to authentic discipleship in any church.

The biblical model for church community is an authentic and healthy transparency that repeatedly points people back to the gospel. It is *never* healthy to try covering sin or hiding it away. Even God, who is sinless and perfect, makes no attempt to conceal the reality of sin. When my son was struggling so much, one of the elders at my church pointed out how even God's first children — Adam and Eve — sinned extensively. If God's own children sinned, why should I be surprised that mine did as well?

We need to also remember that God calls us to be holy (1 Peter 1:15 – 16). What does holiness look like? It's not what we often picture — a rigid call to faultless perfection, something we can never attain, not through our own efforts anyway. Holiness is the gracious gift of God. It's the freedom we experience from sin's power as we are declared righteous in Christ. It's the joy we now have as we run in the pathways of the Lord's commands (Ps. 119:32). Instead of seeking to hide their sin and project an image of perfection, church leaders need to show people they lead that they too are redeemed sinners growing in the ways of Christlikeness. The overall trajectory of our life is to live set apart for Christ. This comes with the humble recognition that we will never be perfect this side of heaven, yet we also recognize that the Holy Spirit is doing his work and increasing spiritual fruit in our lives. If we model this for the church, then people who struggle on the path of discipleship will have a new model for growing in godliness. This is one reason why God, in his Book, gives us flawed, broken characters. The Bible is filled with the failures and sins of men and women, but those are the very people God saves and uses for his purposes. This should give us hope that he can use us as well.

Leaders need to model for their churches what it means to stumble (James 3:2) and yet remain faithful to the path. When we fall down (and we all do), we get right back up on the road with Jesus' help. We model for the church that we do not "claim to be without sin" and that we do not "deceive ourselves" (1 John 1:5 – 10). Instead we confess sin (appropriately) and point people to the forgiveness and faithful path in the ways of Jesus.

Christ calls us to holiness, authentic holiness. When I talk to other pastors about my decision to be honest about my shortcomings, they sometimes give me funny looks. They tell me they don't want to be vulnerable or authentic. I understand. I didn't want to share either. Yet we must, if we want to make disciples.

The first part of this shift—from informing people to equipping them—begins with the character of the leader, not with what he does. We have an adage for this point: "you can't lead where you don't go, and you can't teach what you don't know" (see 1 Cor. 4:6). It begins with a leader living the life himself or herself—as a disciple of Jesus Christ.

When leaders first hear about this shift, many are tempted to start by leading a small group. They assume that the solution to the problem is to add being authentic to the long list of things they are already doing. But that doesn't work. While it's good for pastors to be part of a small group in which they can be authentic, the change I'm talking about is far more encompassing. The solution is not simply adding one more thing to your to-do list; it requires an inner transformation, a step of faith, a change in the way you see yourself and your relationship to others. It begins by allowing Christ to change you from the inside out.

A pastor must be immersed in the Word of God, yielded to the

Holy Spirit, and in relationship with other people. That last one is usually the trickiest for pastors. They see this directive and think they just need to start meeting with their peers, getting together with other pastors. Again, that may be part of the solution, but I find it most helpful when a pastor is in a regular group with regular people in his own church. Leaders need to see the people they serve as their peers—unless they don't really believe in the priesthood of all believers! Following Christ's example, they choose to meet with a group of ordinary men and be real with them.

Though it may sound strange at first, we've found that one of the best things a church planter or pastor can do to grasp the power of vulnerability is to be involved in a quality twelve-step program. The early church didn't have twelve-step programs, because their authenticity with one another made them unnecessary. But today, if a person has a problem or a struggle with an addiction, one of the first places he or she turns is to a twelve-step program. Sadly, one of the last places many look is to the church. I am praying that this will change. I've found that disciple-making churches often produce an environment that is more akin to a twelve-step program than to the educational or entertainment culture that currently defines many churches. Most church leaders would do well to consider establishing the program *Celebrate Recovery* as an important step in changing the overall culture of their church toward one that makes disciples.

One final caution here, particularly to pastors who preach each Sunday. I see many pastors who are convicted by their need to be more authentic, and they immediately go back to their churches the next Sunday and start spilling all their inner secrets from the pulpit. Again, that's not what I'm talking about. A pastor needs to be genuine at all levels of relationship, but not all kinds of relationships require the same amount of disclosure. A pastor can be open and honest at every level of ministry, but he does not need to be equally vulnerable at every level of relationship. Some things are best shared by a pastor with those in close relationship with him.

When we look at Jesus' model of relational discipleship, we find that he discipled people in different relational environments, with the first typically being the most impactful.[23] Wise church planters and leaders will seek to find ways to build their churches with each of these categories in mind.[24]

The four relational environments are:

1. *Intimate Discipling Relationships (one leader interacting with two or three people).* Jesus was relationally closest to three disciples—Peter, James, and John—and he invested his highest-quality time in them. One of them, John, even held the title of "the disciple whom Jesus loved" (John 21:20). These men were often privileged to receive information and experience situations that other disciples weren't. Jesus intentionally nurtured, challenged, and relied on these men.

   There were some events that they alone were allowed to witness. For instance, it was these three who were present with Jesus during the transfiguration. When Jesus raised a girl from the dead, Peter, James, and John were the ones there to see it. And the night before his crucifixion, Jesus asked these three men to join him in prayer in the garden of Gethsemane. He shared with them that his soul was grieved to the point of death. With these three men, Jesus modeled the deepest level of intentional relational discipleship. His wisdom and methodology had a huge impact on them. After his ascension, these three became the leaders of the early church.

   In a like manner, wise church planters and pastors will typically find their most effective discipleship through mentoring two to three key leaders. This is what we see in the examples of Moses and Joshua, Elijah and Elisha, and Paul and Timothy (and Titus). In a church plant, these key disciples will likely be your small group leaders, key staff members, or first elders and deacons.

2. *Personal Discipling Relationships (one leader interacting with ten to twelve people).* The second category of relational discipleship involves a larger group of ten to twelve people whom you personally disciple. Jesus had personal relationships with his twelve disciples. Not all of them were *intimately* close to him, but they still received quality relationship and spent regular time with him. Jesus' work with the Twelve was the focus

of much of his ministry and discipleship while on earth. He poured into their lives, and they learned how to minister with him to others.

Jesus' relationship with the Twelve is a good approximation to what we call small groups in our local church. At this level of relationship, a disciple maker has a personal relationship with about twelve people. He can know them, their personal lives and struggles, and help them follow Jesus in that real-life context. The small group leader may have an apprentice whom he disciples in a more intimate relationship, one of his two or three key disciples from the first category. Together they care for the rest of the group.

3. *Social Discipling Relationships (one leader interacting with up to 120 people).* In this category of relational discipleship, we see a leader interacting with a larger group of people. Jesus had significant social relationships with people like Mary, Martha, and Lazarus. He also had a relationship with a group referred to as "the seventy-two" (Luke 10:17). We do not know much about this group, other than that Jesus invested time in these men before he sent them out to minister in his name. It may be that the seventy-two were also part of the 120 who later met in the upper room when the Holy Spirit came down on the day of Pentecost. At this level of relationship, people usually know each other by name, and they may know a few personal details about one other. Throughout history, most churches have been about this size.

This is an important category to keep in mind when you are shifting to a more discipleship focus in your church. In many ways, this is the ideal size for a group of people who want to work together in service and mission. Keep in mind that within a group this big, there will also be groups of ten to twelve, as well as more intimate relationships between people (groups of three).

4. *Public Discipling Relationships (one leader interacting with larger crowds of people).* In this fourth category of relational discipleship, a leader interacts with a larger crowd of people

in a public relationship. This is the level at which Jesus discipled people publicly, speaking to various sizes of crowds and sharing teaching like the Sermon on the Mount. At this level, Jesus would teach God's Word and explain the realities of God's kingdom. Most people passively listened to him, yet his words powerfully transformed minds and hearts. Jesus shared some things with the crowds, but not everything that he shared with the smaller groups.

This is the level at which crowds of people came together "as a church" in the New Testament (Acts 2:42–47; 1 Cor. 11:17–14:40). The people would meet together in the temple courts. They would share Communion, words of encouragement, teaching, special songs, and the like (1 Cor. 14:26). This level of relational discipleship is often where church leaders will set the vision, imparting the basic DNA of what it means to follow Jesus. This is also where leaders and gifted teachers will speak about authenticity, transparency, and, most important, a commitment to Jesus and the cross. Public gatherings are an important category for relational discipleship, as long as they are authentic and Christ-centered. At this level, pastors can model, in their teaching and personal stories, what it means to be a Christian. There is good research to show that this is the level at which many lost people first learn what it means to be a disciple of Jesus.[25]

These four categories of relational environments are interrelated to one another in churches that are making disciples. Although the smaller-size groups are more effective at equipping disciples, all four discipling relationships are important components of a disciple-making church. We need to remember that relational shaping happens at all levels. For instance, when I walk through the lobby of our church after a weekend service, I'm engaging with people at the public level. I'm going to shake a lot of hands and hug a lot of people, but it's very seldom that I'll end up sharing intimate details of my life with the people I meet. I simply want those who attend to get a taste of what our church is like if they choose to get more relationally involved.

My time for in-depth sharing is with my small group or with my men's group or when I meet with a close friend, a mentor, or my accountability partner.

Knowing that I don't need to be close friends with everybody takes the pressure off me a bit. I don't feel the need to go to the pulpit and publicly spill everything I'm struggling with (which is not all that appropriate and can even be dangerous). Being involved in relationships at each of these levels also frees me from feeling like I have to be the one who cares for each person in our church. I know there is a structure in place to help people get connected in close, intimate relationships. I know there are ways for them to develop friendships and get better acquainted with others in the church. And yes, I still try to be authentic and personal when I preach. Even vulnerable at times. But no, I don't need to share every detail about my life with everyone who visits our church. I might let people know that on the way to church I had an argument with my wife. I know that in sharing a struggle like this, I can better relate to anyone who has argued with someone they love. What I am really telling them is that if they are struggling with this too, then this church is a place where they are welcome to struggle! When I meet with my small group, I'll probably share the details of the argument with them, inviting them to challenge me and pray for me in these personal matters.

THE PLACE TO START

Here is the simplest way to start being more authentic: begin at the most intimate levels. This doesn't start in the pulpit. Begin with your close friends, with an accountability partner. If you don't have one, then this is a problem that needs to be dealt with first. Share some of your struggles with your small group or your leadership team. Take small steps to begin creating a culture that graciously accepts being open and honest about sin and struggle. Then, when you have the support and understanding of people around you, you can branch out to the crowds.

This is where the shift from informing people to equipping them begins. It starts with honest, humble leaders who are living out in their personal relationships what they want other people to live out in theirs. So begin there, in your closest relationships. Model authenticity. Be vulnerable. Share your struggle. Create an environment in the teams you lead that avoids starting on your task list (we all have them and they can be long) before you start on the relational and shepherding discussion. That's the place to start.

But it doesn't end there. Even if you are modeling this type of relationship, it doesn't mean that your job description frees you to focus on equipping others. So how does a pastor transition the specific tasks he performs as he tries to shift from being an informer to being an equipper? What does he actually do? We'll look at the answer to this question in the next chapter.

KEY POINTS

- As a church leader, particularly as a senior or lead pastor, you set the tone for what spiritual maturity looks like in your congregation. You don't just teach about maturity when you speak to your congregation. You are also responsible (with the Lord's help) to live in such a way that people can see true discipleship and spiritual maturity in the actions of your life. As the head goes, the body follows.

- If the enemy can cause a leader to live out the wrong definition of discipleship and maturity, then people end up with wrong definitions. For instance, if leaders don't practice biblical love, then the people in the church will use the word *love* but not exhibit it accurately either. Modeling plays such a huge part in parenting and disciple making.

- The key is to be genuine, but that doesn't mean spilling all from the pulpit. Jesus' example shows that he interacted at different levels with different groups of people. For instance, he was much closer to Peter, James, and John (his inner circle), than he was to the multitudes he ministered to. Still, there is a place for authenticity with all people.

Chapter 6

A NEW JOB TITLE: EQUIPPER

What are the specific roles of a disciple-making pastor?

Years ago when I was a college wrestler, I had a coach whom everybody raved about. He was on track to compete in the Olympics, and he could do amazing things on the mat. Yet as good as he was, it might surprise you to hear that I didn't learn much about wrestling from him. He saw his job as his own personal training ground, a way to showcase his own abilities. It soon became clear to me that he wasn't interested in coaching any of us in how to be great wrestlers. He needed us so he could continue his training. In other words, he was primarily interested in his own growth — becoming the best wrestler he could be. The coaching job was simply a way to get paid for his training.

On the other hand, I've had wrestling coaches over the years who saw teaching others how to wrestle as their primary job and calling. These were the men I learned the most from. They created environments and structures in which kids grew in their abilities and confidence. Their job wasn't to perform; it was to coach others — and that made all the difference.

A key verse for pastors and church planters is Ephesians 4:11–13: "Christ himself gave the apostles, the prophets, the evangelists, the pastors and teachers, to equip his people for works of service, so that the body of Christ may be built up until we all reach unity in the faith and in the knowledge of the Son of God and become mature, attaining to the whole measure of the fullness of Christ." Read that verse again if you need to. It tells us that the goal of a church leader (apostles, prophets, evangelists, pastors, and teachers) is to equip people for works of service or ministry so that the body of Christ can be built up. Why? So that we *all* reach unity and spiritual maturity.

Some church leaders see their role as similar to that of a star athlete. They want to excel and lead the team by their own personal achievements. The people on their team exist to fulfill their own personal mission for significance. But leading in the church is more like being a really good coach.[26] A leader's job is to guide and equip the saints so that the entire church becomes a mature community in which disciples flourish. It involves releasing the ministry and gifts of all believers. It's about creating a place where everybody learns to be a minister by growing, serving, and making disciples themselves.

Again, that's the key concept behind this second shift—from *informing* people to *equipping* them.

Ask/Dr. Coleman

If a pastor said to you, "The primary function of my job is to impart knowledge," how would you answer him or help clarify that statement?

Well, that statement could be interpreted different ways. If he's talking about imparting the knowledge of Christ, of the Word, of experiencing truth, that's one thing. A pastor is a teacher and should be imparting knowledge. In fact, the words *pastor* and *teacher* in Ephesians 4 are used without a definite article between them, which leads many to believe it's the same office. However you want to interpret the two words, they're certainly closely related. A pastor should be a teacher.

Yet a pastor's primary job is to shepherd the sheep. This means to lead them in the way of truth. You lead them by example, not just by imparting knowledge. You let them see the knowledge incarnate. An example goes a lot farther than a mere explanation. Hopefully, people see the example of Christ in your life.

Of course, we all fall short of the example Christ sets before us. Nevertheless, that is what we aspire to be, just as Paul said, "Be imitators of me, as I am of Christ" (1 Cor. 11:1 ESV). Now, that's pretty strong language, and it certainly puts us as leaders on the spot. But for good or ill, we are an example to people who follow us.

THE FOUNDATIONS OF EQUIPPING

Some time ago I worked with a large church in which the senior pastor was out for a jog one day and suffered a heart attack. He lived, thank God, but during the six months or so it took for him to recover, the attendance at the church dropped by half. Quite literally, thousands of people just stopped coming to the weekend services. The senior pastor came to me, along with his executive pastor and his small groups pastor, and he admitted that he had built his church around an entertainment model, relying on music, technology, and his own personality and ability to teach. The result was a one-man star attraction, and when he wasn't around anymore, the people just moved on.

I wish this were an isolated story. I can't tell you how many churches we work with that are set up this way or are unconsciously trying to become like this. Their emphasis and methodology are misplaced.

And that's what needs to shift.

If a church *emphasizes* the wrong things and then uses the wrong *methodologies* to reach its goals, the result will not be fruitful, mature disciples. Making this shift means moving from a leader who believes it's his job to inform other people about how to live the Christian life to a leader who equips people to live out the ministry of all believers moving forward in spiritual maturity. It's about shifting the spotlight from the pastor as the star player to the pastor as the head coach. So take a moment to consider: professional athlete or coach? What kind of spiritual leader are you?

- As a professional athlete, you have all eyes on you, watching you perform. You entertain. You inspire. The pressure is on you.
- As a coach, you empower other people to work together as a team. Your role is to equip, nurture, exhort, and train. You release and deploy other people to do the boots-on-the-ground work of disciple making.

THE ROLE OF THE WEEKEND SERVICE

Sometimes when people hear me say this, they immediately jump three steps down the line and think I'm criticizing their Sunday services. They think I'm opposed to having solid, dynamic Bible teaching from the pulpit.

But I'm not.

In our Relational Discipleship network of churches, we don't downplay the need for a quality Bible-based message at the weekend service. We believe that the sermon is important and has a purpose. We believe it is important to regularly and thoroughly teach the Bible to our people. Good things can happen in large-group settings that can't happen in small ones, and when we come to church each weekend, it's exciting to see large numbers of people committed to the same thing. It enables us to see that we are part of a bigger movement. When we listen to a gifted Bible teacher, we come away inspired, encouraged, and ready for action.

But we do not depend on the weekend service to do the *primary* work of what we're seeking to accomplish as a church. Jesus didn't use the methodology of preaching to the crowds as his core means of making disciples, so why should we? One of the obvious factors that limits a weekend service's effectiveness is that a sermon happens only once a week. Many Christians attend church fewer than two times a month.[27] Can you imagine trying to teach algebra to a university student if he were one of eighty students in your classroom and he showed up for class only every other week? If we place the bulk of our resources into the weekend services, is it any wonder that so many Christians today don't have a biblical worldview? Especially when they are being fed the world's way of seeing things every day on television, in movies, and from friends. So as important as the sermon and the weekend service are, we don't pour all (or even the bulk) of our resources into that one component.

Consider a church that has an attractional focus and uses methodology focused on inspiration. In this church, a leader will typically focus on doing biblical evangelism by designing church services that attract people. Helping people make decisions for Christ is the primary goal for these church leaders, and it is assumed that discipleship will naturally happen through church attendance or participation in one of the church's programs.

Experience has shown that some of the assumptions of the attractional church can be misguided. Inevitably, a variety of problems will result, even when the stated goal is to make mature believers. The weekend messages will typically be geared toward seekers and less mature believers, so they won't be designed to challenge people to grow more deeply in their faith. Instead they will focus on introducing people to Jesus. To be sure, introductions to Christ have their place, but if they are all that a Christian hears, then these messages are unlikely to lead to lasting spiritual maturity. The attractional model is designed to lead people to an emotional response — to make a decision — so if this is always the goal, those who come, over time, will often believe that Christianity is about emotion rather than sometimes being an act of obedience, whether you feel like it or not. Attractional models will not take into account that people need spiritual parenting, and because they don't, it doesn't often happen. The more mature believers will not be satisfied with just milk every week and will eventually funnel out. Not only are they not learning as much as they desire, but they are not being intentionally used in the lives of the less mature. In this case, you are left with immature people who are on fire for a while, but eventually will get bored with even the best shows. A church may have ten thousand people showing up each Sunday, but the numbers can be deceptive. Are disciples actually being made? How many of the ten thousand are consistently growing and maturing in their faith? That's the real question we want to ask.[28]

So how can we as church leaders ensure that we're involved in the right tasks and using the right methodologies? Again, the answer seems obvious. We look to Jesus.

THE LEADERSHIP OF JESUS

Simply put, Jesus was the *master* disciple maker.

Jesus' lifestyle first and foremost reflected a close relationship with his Father. As we just described, beyond that, he was personally connected to the twelve disciples, and he had a more intimate relationship with three of them. He discipled them by allowing them to see him making tough decisions, to see how he responded to hurting people or to enemies as well. He asked them to pray with him when he was grieved to the point of death (Matt. 26:36–38). While we need to be careful in assuming that we should do everything Jesus did, much of what he did serves as an example to us. Christlikeness is the goal of discipleship, and looking at Jesus' life helps us better understand what it means to be a mature believer. Before Jesus focused on *doing* something, he focused on *being* in relationship with God and with his disciples.

To accomplish his mission, Jesus didn't focus on the tasks of ministry alone or even the majority of the time (preaching, healing, teaching, and so on). He would often lead his disciples away from the crowd to rest. Looking at his life, we begin to see that fruitfulness in ministry is not just a matter of rolling up your sleeves and working harder, especially if you're doing things in an ineffective manner. Jesus used a method, and it is a method we would be wise to adopt. Too many church leaders wrongly think that if they just had another day of the week to do what they're already doing, or if they could just hire another staff person to help spread the work around, or if they could just motivate more volunteers to fill in the gaps, then all would be okay with their church. And while sometimes those things are integral components of the overall solution, the real solution is working smarter at the wisest thing.

This means shifting how we think about our job, our calling as a pastor or leader. It means that being an effective church leader involves:

- Discovering what the right goal is: making disciples, not just converts
- Correctly defining what a disciple is: someone who follows Jesus, is transformed by Jesus, and joins Jesus on his mission
- Using the right methodology: intentional, biblical, relational environments
- Producing the intended results: disciples who are spiritually and relationally healthy and are continually making more disciples

The bottom line is that a leader is *not* following Jesus' example if he's not personally involved in the work of making disciples in every aspect. Many pastors might say, "I will take on the preaching aspect of the job," but allow others to do the relational discipleship stuff. However, that is not what Jesus or Paul did (or any other example in Scripture). If a pastor is not developing and nurturing key relationships in which he is equipping others to follow Jesus, then he's not doing what Jesus modeled for him to do. A pastor or teacher might be filled with lots of head knowledge, might have a tremendous zeal for world missions, or might be busy working at any number of tasks required to run a church, but any of these, taken alone, is incomplete.

THE FOUR MAIN ROLES OF A DISCIPLE-MAKING PASTOR

If you want to make the shift from informing to equipping and be a disciple-making pastor, your ministry needs to revolve around the following four main roles.

1. An Authentic Disciple

We've already talked about this in the previous chapter, so I'll just summarize by reminding you that biblical leadership begins with who we are and our walk with God. There is an old saying: "Who you are thunders so loud that it drowns out your words." Pastors must learn to walk with God daily. This is why church leaders are men of prayer, Bible study, and the inner life of the spirit. When we walk authentically with God, it gives legitimacy to our teaching and leadership.

It is especially important to live out the life of an authentic disciple with our families. Too many church leaders neglect the most important mission field of all—their own homes. When we walk with God together with our families, this becomes the daily testing ground that authenticates the teaching and leading we do in the church.

2. A Discipleship-System Builder

A church leader, especially one involved in church planting or pastoring, is not just a disciple or even just a disciple maker. A disciple is a person who follows Jesus, is transformed by Jesus, and joins Jesus on his mission; that's the job of every believer. A disciple maker makes disciples. Every Christian has that job. A pastor is more than that. He has been given the task of leading a church in which he is to create a system in which people are taught how to be disciples. In other words, he and his team are called to lead in the development of a church-wide system that will make disciples who make disciples. Leadership (or administration, as it is called in Scripture) is a responsibility that is broader than just discipling others or leading a small group. Church planters should follow Timothy and Titus and build churches that serve as the "household of God" and the "pillar and buttress of the truth" (1 Tim. 3:14–16 ESV). Included in Paul's instructions to Timothy was the call to develop disciple-making leaders and systems. Paul writes about this in 2 Timothy 2:2: "The things you have heard me say in the presence of many witnesses entrust to reliable people who will also be qualified to teach others."

As a church leader, your job is to create the community-wide system in which people can be involved in relational environments for the purpose of discipleship. You are an overseer of a disciple-making community.

In later chapters, we'll talk more about how to build these systems, so right now I'm not going to go into specific details about what these structures look like. At this point, it's about having the right understanding—the proper mindset. You need to see yourself as a systems developer or as a coach who is coaching his players. You may not know how to do that. This is why God builds teams of leaders who work together to fill in the gaps. We work together and are responsible for developing the program in which the team is trained, inspired, encouraged, challenged, and fully developed.

Here are some examples of ineffective leadership styles contrasted with more effective leadership styles. Ineffective ministry practices do not follow the pattern set by Ephesians 4. Effective ministry practices are grounded in both the Ephesians 4 coaching mindset (equipping ministry) and the understanding that ministry is the responsibility of all believers, not just a specialized few. Church leaders are to be equipper-coaches, and the people are the ministers. Both of these concepts are bound together. The ministry of all believers is just as important as the coaching role of leaders.

Ineffective: Since I'm trained in the Bible and theology, I'm the primary one at my church who should teach the Bible.

Effective: Since I'm trained in the Bible and theology, I can create support systems in my church that teach others how to teach the Bible in relational contexts.

Ineffective: The church pays me to take care of the congregation. That means if anyone in my congregation gets sick, I need to go visit that person.

Effective: God calls me to take care of the congregation. That means I create small groups and raise up leaders in my congregation who can go visit people when they get sick.

Ineffective: I need to be highly effective, creative, and entertaining in the pulpit so I can draw a large crowd and inform people about what the Bible says.

Effective: I need to be effective, creative, biblically based, and yes, even entertaining in the pulpit so I can effectively communicate the gospel to the lost and then get people connected with other disciple makers in the church so everyone engages in the work of the ministry.

Ineffective: I'm the church's leader, so the congregation needs me to be present each week to open the children's meetings with prayer.

Effective: I'm the church's leader, and I'm in the process of training other leaders to effectively disciple children via the weekly children's gatherings. That means they can open the meeting with prayer. I may or may not be there, depending on my schedule.

Ineffective: I'm the minister. This means I need to be the person ministering to the needs of the people in the congregation.

Effective: I'm to be the equipper or coach of the people in the church. They are the ones ministering to the needs of the people. The more effective I am in my job, the more we will develop ministers, and the more service and good work will be done by the church.

Ask Dr. Coleman

What is the primary role of the pastor in the disciple-making process?

His life should illustrate what it means to be a disciple maker. I'm afraid that's not true of all pastors. Pastors are so busy preparing for their sermons and administering the various activities of the church, they're hardly known by the people in any personal way. But the pastor should convey to his congregation that with a few people, he's investing largely of his life. A pastor can't let everybody in the congregation see what he's doing, but to a measure, he can let a few people know. He should be careful to protect time for those people.

This is the principle of selection I mention in my book. When it comes down to really imparting your life to a person, you can't do that with very many people at the same time. Thankfully, you can do this almost every day with your family while your children are growing up—that's the ideal place that God gives everyone to disciple.

When a pastor is invested in a few, word gets around, and the congregation can make the association with what he teaches. Hopefully, too, they will see the fruit of that closeness in development of leadership that finds expression in the work of the church.

Yes, the pastor has a level of vulnerability with those persons close to him. Some pastors feel threatened by this concept. For if you as pastor get too close to people, they'll see what's wrong with you. They'll see how you have failed and how you need to make corrections. Hopefully, we have some persons close enough to us who'll help us along the way. You need somebody who'll be honest with you.

Disciple making is not only God's plan for evangelizing the world; it's his plan to encourage the sanctification of the church. You do that by being close enough to people who will affirm you, exhort you, and point out to you where you're failing, while also helping you see the possibilities of grace in your life.

3. A Developer of Leaders

The third main role of a church planter or pastor in a disciple-making church is that of a developer of leaders. Everyone is a disciple and should grow into an effective disciple maker, but not everyone is gifted as a leader. A church planter or pastoral leadership team should identify emerging, gifted leaders and help them grow. But how do you find leaders? Some pastors lament the lack of leaders in their church. But I believe that for the most part, the leaders are already there in the body; they are just undeveloped or overlooked. God promises that he will supply all we need in terms of gifted people to complete the mission he gave us (see Matt. 16:18; Rom. 12:4–8; Phil. 4:19).[29]

So we really face three problems. First, most leaders are too busy trying to do the work in the church themselves, and they don't have time to see and develop the leaders God has sent them. The machine needs feeding, and they have to feed it — preaching every week, planning everything, meeting every person who needs counseling, going to the hospital, doing weddings and funerals. This keeps them from noticing the undeveloped people God has sent them.

The second problem is that church leaders are looking for already-developed leaders. They don't see the potential in their midst because it's not yet visible. In my first book, *Church Is a Team Sport*, I used the analogy of the difference between a high school coach and a college coach. A college coach goes all over the country looking for developed and talented players, and then he offers them scholarships to come and play for him. But a high school coach needs to get his players from within his own school district. Every once in a while, a talented kid will move in, but that seldom happens. If you want to win at the high school level, you must create a program that develops an athlete from the kids program to the junior high level and finally to the high school level. You develop the students and build your team with what you have, from where you are. As kids graduate, they may come back to plug into some of the coaching roles, and over time a winning program emerges. Most pastors I know act more like college coaches. They are focused on looking for the developed players rather than developing people in their own church because they are too busy playing every position on the team to develop anyone.

Third, pastors tend to look for a person who can do everything — an all-star player, if you will — rather than a person who can play a specific position on a great team. I don't believe there is anyone who can do it all. That's why we need the whole body of Christ. If you start thinking of building effective teams that work well together, it changes what you look for in developing a good leader. Rather than looking for the perfect leader, you look for people who understand their own weaknesses and can join your leadership team, serving in a way that works well with others on the team.

Not everyone can lead thousands of people, but most can lead a group of three or ten. In a good church system, you need all kinds of leaders who have different leadership capabilities. We know that God gives specific gifts to people in the church in order to help the church work together effectively. Romans 12 and 1 Corinthians 12, among other passages, tell us that God gives spiritual gifts to all believers. One person is given the gift of wisdom, another is strong in faith, another receives the gift of leadership. All gifts work together for the overall good of the church, in the same way that the various parts of a human body come together and function as a unit.

One of the primary spiritual gifts we need in the church is the gift of administration (leadership). In our context, we equate this gift with organizing, which is a leadership gift. It's the ability to spiritually manage other people and help them journey in a good direction. This is the type of leader that pastors need to seek out, raise up, and deploy. Churches in the Relational Discipleship Network make it a practice to develop people who are spiritually mature and who have the spiritual gift of leadership. Too often, though, churches accept those with proven leadership abilities in the secular world and make them leaders in the church without ever assessing where they are in terms of spiritual growth. The bottom line in the world of business is money — the number of products sold, share value, percentage of market influenced, and volume of customers. So when gifted but spiritually immature leaders are placed in leadership positions in church, they tend to think in the same terms: giving, attendance, salvation statistics, size of buildings. But the bottom line in God's church is *discipleship* — people following Jesus, being transformed by Jesus, and joining Jesus on his mission. The evaluation criteria is different. That's why we need to make sure we are measuring the right things in the right way.

If we discern that a person is a leader, we must help that person grow through the spiritual stages of development, training them to become the kind of organizational leader God wants them to be. Leadership development is similar to discipleship, but it is different. Some people mature to the point where they are spiritual parents, but they are not necessarily gifted or effective in church leadership positions. For example, we can all think of people who have done a great job in discipling their children, but they are not very effective at leading a small group or administrating a ministry. At our church, we know of many who made great small group leaders (they could disciple people) but were not good coaches of small group leaders.

Leadership development in a church will focus on people who have developed spiritually to the point where they are in the young adult or spiritual parent phase, or are now moving into those phases. We want to make sure that those we move into leadership positions have the spiritual maturity necessary to take on these added responsibilities. A spiritual young adult has grown beyond self-focus to being genuinely more concerned about what the Lord wants.

When developing apprentices and leaders, we follow something like the formula promoted by Dave Ferguson and John Ferguson in their book *Exponential*.[30] This leadership apprentice model can be replicated in every ministry in a church, from hospital visitation to children's ministry to the role of a senior pastor (training an associate or church planter).

I do. You watch. We talk.

I do. You help. We talk.

You do. I help. We talk.

You do. I watch. We talk.

You do. Someone else watches.

Jesus modeled something similar to this when he was working with the disciples, and a careful review of Paul's writings will show that he did something like this with Timothy and Titus. A church leader needs a simple but effective model like this to successfully develop leaders.

4. A Vision Caster

A church leader must also be able to cast the vision that creates the disciple-making culture of the church. He not only makes it clear that everyone is to be involved in making disciples; he constantly points people to the method — relational environments — for doing this. That means sharing the vision from the pulpit and at every opportunity he has with the other leaders and the people in the church. He is continually telling them, "This is our vision, this is where we're going, this is what we're about." Every sermon is both a teaching opportunity and a vision-casting opportunity, a way of showing people what God has called the church to be and to do.

And what is that vision?

The vision is that the church's primary mission is to create disciples who create other disciples, just as Jesus intended us to do. It's helping people see that the church isn't a social club, it's not a hospital, it's not a university, and it's not a big show. The church is a community that is developing people who follow Jesus, are changed by Jesus, and then join Jesus on his mission. A pastor needs to state that vision, then state it again and again and again. And then, just when he thinks people are getting tired of hearing the vision, he needs to repeat it some more. People forget. People drift in their thinking. People get new ideas and want to explore different directions in a church. But a pastor needs to continually cast vision — the same vision.

Continual vision casting is particularly necessary when a pastor meets with other leaders in the church. Discipling others can be hard work. Leaders get tired, discouraged, and beat up. A pastor needs to continually remind and encourage his leaders to stay the course — keep making disciples who make other disciples.

One strategic tool in the vision-casting process is the tool of celebration. What you celebrate, your people will aspire to. A celebration is really the way to reaffirm what you measure as most important. Many churches celebrate attendance, money given, building program benchmarks, and numbers of new conversions. We try to celebrate conversions as well, but we also celebrate how many people are getting connected, how many people are starting to serve, and how many people are starting to lead as disciple makers. What a church measures is indicative of that church's vision.

Not only does the pastor need to cast the vision and repeat it, but he needs to continually guard the vision as well. New ideas emerge all the time, some that are profitable, some that are not, and once a system to create disciples is up and running, a church leader will need to defend that system and constantly reinforce it, protecting the system against vision drift. This means constantly beating the drum. The devil is always working to destroy effective systems. When other ideas come along, a pastor must decide if the church really needs them. He must discern if an open door is something from God or merely somebody else's idea of what the church should do. Will this new idea or concept lead to making disciples, or will it take energy away from the main thing?

FROM INFORMING TO EQUIPPING

In the previous two chapters, we talked about the necessity of leadership in the disciple-making process. As the head leads, the body follows, and if we want churches to be as effective as they can be, church leaders must be fully committed and involved in shaping the process. As we've seen, leaders need to make a shift from informing congregations to equipping them. We want to raise up people for works of service so that the body of Christ may be built up. Our goal is unity in the faith and in the knowledge of the Son of God. We want people to become spiritually mature, attaining to the whole measure of the fullness of Christ.

And if you're a leader, this process starts with you. Bobby Harrington planted the church he leads outside Nashville in 1998 without knowledge of these shifts. At first he planted an attractional church. Then, several years ago, we began spending time together, and he asked me to help him change the DNA of the church so that it would be more effective at making disciples who make disciples. The process we followed is basically the shifts we are discussing in this book (which is why he is helping me describe them to you!).

Bobby recalls that after making his own personal commitment to live out intentional relational discipleship as a leader (to be what you want others to be), the hardest shift he had to make was to reposition the leadership and structure of the whole church around this approach. Yes, it is easier to plant new churches with this DNA from the beginning, but Bobby (and other leaders in the Relational

Discipleship Network) will tell you that if you are willing to do a lot of hard work and endure some or even a lot of difficulties (and be patient), this *can* be done in an established church as well. In fact, Bobby and others like him believe that faithfulness to Jesus' method, Jesus' teaching, and Jesus' emphasis on love and relationships leaves them no other choice. They have to be about the mission of making disciples who make disciples.

They are patiently rebuilding the DNA of their churches along these lines. Bobby is an advocate of prayer, collaboration, honest evaluation from his team, and steely determination on the road through these shifts. He estimates that his church is most of the way through all this, which is especially difficult in an area as traditional and highly churched as the greater Nashville area, but he is glad that they are making the transition. It has been difficult, but he believes it is worth it.

Our hope in writing this book is that his example and the example of other churches in the Relational Discipleship Network (and in other contexts) will inspire and encourage you. You *can* make these shifts. If you understand what we are saying in the previous two chapters and believe in the mission of making disciples, you are well on your way. We have now looked at two of the shifts that will get you started, but the remaining three are key to completing a successful transition.

KEY POINTS

- A key passage for church planters and pastors is Ephesians 4:11 – 13. The goal of a church leader is to equip people so that the body of Christ can be built up and we all reach unity and spiritual maturity. Being a church leader is much less like being a star athlete and much more like being a great coach.
- As a church leader, your job is to create an overall system in which people can be placed into environments where they are discipled. As a pastor, you are not discipling everybody yourself. Rather, you are creating a system in which everybody in your church can be discipled.

- A strong commitment to the ministry of all believers is equally as important as the role of the pastor as an equipper-coach in a disciple-making church.
- Continual vision casting is key when a pastor meets with other leaders in the church. The work of discipling others can be hard. Leaders get tired, discouraged, and beat up. A pastor needs to continually remind and encourage his leaders to stay the course, to keep making disciples who make other disciples.

SHIFT

3

From Program
to Purpose

Chapter 7

COMPONENTS OF PERSON-TO-PERSON DISCIPLESHIP

What's the true role of the church?

A friend just returned from the Middle East. While there, he met with an Arab Christian pastor who is keenly committed to discipleship. Since his goal is to follow Jesus' method of discipleship, he has created a church that emphasizes different relational environments for discipleship. He has created a church in which people are discipled publicly and from house to house (Acts 20:20).

Good thing, because a young woman and her mother just gave their lives to Christ out of a Muslim and Bedouin background. When the Muslims heard of their conversion, they threatened to burn down the church building and harm the church leaders if she ever attended a public gathering there. Tough stuff! But because the church is effective at making disciples from house to house, their exclusion from the public gathering of the church will not be a huge barrier to their growth.

What would happen to most churches in North America today if people could meet only in houses, not publicly? This question helps us to see how much we rely on programs instead of discipleship through personal relationships.

133

THE IMPORTANCE OF RELATIONAL ENVIRONMENTS

The third shift that churches need to make is to foster a culture of personalized discipleship. It's a change from program-based, informational environments to hands-on training in relational environments. It's a shift from program to purpose, and it begins by asking the question, What is the true role of the church?

As I wrote earlier, it is true that Jesus ministered by speaking to large numbers of people, and he was very engaged in serving people, showing people the reality of God's kingdom. And there are times when we should follow his example and hold large teaching gatherings or be involved in service and ministries that transform communities. But as we have said, neither of these methodologies fully captures how Jesus made disciples — through *relationships*.

When Jesus said to go and make disciples, he defined his methodology by his own example. Jesus' methodology was more involved than just standing in front of people and teaching them biblical truth. He walked alongside people, having conversations with them through the normal course of each day, holding people accountable, and demonstrating spiritual truth to them directly. We place such a high importance on relational environments because that's the methodology Jesus used — and because it worked!

We recognize that in our culture today, it's a challenge to be relational the way Jesus was with the people of his day. Most people today lead busy lives in which they are physically separated from other people. Some work in cubicles and rarely see their coworkers. Times have changed from the day when most people worked in a town with a central location where they would meet their neighbors or see them on a daily basis. This means that we need to be creative as we seek to overcome today's proximity problems. We know that proximity is essential to the learning process. To impart truth to your children, you need to be around them on a regular basis. Proximity allows space and time for unplanned, teachable moments. The same is true in the discipleship process. Regular interaction with caring, biblically trained leaders prompts spiritual growth.

We find that many pastors balk at this teaching. They immediately see the challenges and despair of the changes required. They question the need for these relational environments and wonder if this turns the church into a glorified social club. Some sarcastically wonder, Why even bother preaching? Why not just gather everyone together and have a potluck each week?

These are actually good questions to ask, regardless of the tone behind them. The key difference between biblical relational environments and mere social gatherings is a focus on the Word and the intentionality behind the gathering. When we talk about small groups, we present a very specific type of small group to people, with a clear purpose for meeting. We don't advocate small groups simply for the sake of hanging out and getting to know people; we present small group time as an intentional gathering led by a spiritually mature person who understands that his or her job is to help people grow as disciples of Jesus. Now, both in and around a small group, we encourage the development of relationships that extend far beyond this weekly meeting. I go hunting with the men in my small group, and we often have amazing and powerful conversations about our lives. We have dinner together, and our families go camping together. We typically talk several times a week. The relationships that begin in our small group go far beyond the meeting time. People who once were isolated and separate from one another are beginning to experience what it means to be a Christian, and they are learning how Jesus and his Word affects every part of their lives.

This is what we mean by a shift from *program* to *purpose*. As any pastor can tell you, a small group, in and of itself, can become just another program of the church. I call small groups without purpose "flesh bombs." When you get people together who are not growing spiritually and are not being led by spiritual parents, you have a flesh bomb whose fuse is already lit. But a small group designed specifically to promote discipleship has a clear purpose. We define this purpose by saying that a small group must display the following characteristics. It should be

- Bible-centered;
- intentionally directing people to the goal of spiritual maturity;
- a place where people can honestly talk about their lives and work out what it means to follow Jesus.

This is about more than a seven o'clock to nine o'clock commitment each Wednesday night. While there must be a specific time for the group to meet, we should understand that the group exists as a means to developing relationships with people, for the purpose of discipleship. During the study time, the group will dive into the Word and pray together. Later in the week, some members of the group might spend time together drinking coffee and talking about their work or their marriages. Two or three men from the group might start an accountability gathering in which they really talk about their common struggles. Three wives might get together so their kids can play while the parents get some adult time praying together. The home group members may plan times in the summer when they go camping together or go fishing on the weekend. While the meeting times provide regularity and structure, the real goal is relational growth, following Christ together.

Leaders of groups will seek to help people grow and learn the ways of Jesus. A leader will help those who are more mature invest in those who are just beginning or struggling in their walk with God. The leader knows where each person needs to get to and seeks to guide the entire group to maturity. In the meantime, he or she is looking to see who God might be calling to become the apprentice of the group and eventually a leader. The leader will watch to see if someone starts to drift, and he will seek out the strays and draw them back into fellowship with the group. He will help each person in the group figure out how God made them and then help them get connected to a place to serve in the larger body. Some will have a passion for kids and others for missions, but every mature leader knows that each person has been saved for a purpose, and he desires to help them live out that purpose.

Ask/Dr. Coleman

When we talk about programs in the church, we say that Jesus' primary method of making disciples was not to attract a big crowd but rather to invest in a smaller, limited number of people. Please discuss.

Yes, you're talking about Jesus' primary method. His goal was always to raise up people from all nations to the glory of God. His methodology was to make disciples who in turn would make other disciples.

Even though Jesus preached to crowds, sometimes numbering in the thousands, that wasn't his primary disciple-making method. If you read the Gospels carefully, he's spending most of his time with a small handful of people, his disciples. That's where the great teaching comes through. And this method increases, particularly in the third and last year of his ministry. That's where he invests heavily.

Here again the principle of selection comes into prominence. As your ministry expands, the pressures and demands of a church increase. If you're not careful, you can go to this meeting, and teach that class, and visit the Sunday school party, and wind up spending your life carrying on a program, and never reproduce disciples. That's what you have to watch. It's difficult to keep that perspective.

WHY ARE PEOPLE SO IMPORTANT TO THE PROCESS?

We've mentioned before how there are three necessary components to the disciple-making process — the Word of God, the Spirit of God, and the people of God. These three components work together to bring about spiritual maturity in people's lives.

Let's examine the roles of the Word of God and the Spirit of God first. Both are vitally important, and we need to continually remind ourselves of that truth. Then we will examine the importance of the people of God, looking at this a bit more in depth, as it's often the most overlooked of the three components.

1. The Importance of the Word of God

I've seen small groups that are nothing more than social gatherings in which Christians get together for fellowship, for dinner or dessert, or to hang out and watch a movie together. These gatherings aren't wrong or evil. They're important in the overall scheme of doing life together. Humans are social beings, so hanging out is important. But these gatherings aren't the type of small groups that you can use to develop a disciple-making church. Similarly, I've seen small groups that teach a steady diet of "hot topics" or "important life lessons." Some of the lessons are Bible-centered, but others are more aligned with humanism or self-help philosophies than with the Word of God. I have also seen groups that get together to share their struggles and pray together. But more often than not, they don't get down to much praying, and they tend to do a lot of affirming without much direction from God's Word.

The Bible mandates the need for us to be firmly grounded in biblical truth. Second Timothy 4:3–4 says, "The time is coming when people will not endure sound teaching, but having itching ears they will accumulate for themselves teachers to suit their own passions, and will turn away from listening to the truth and wander off into myths" (ESV). Because we are prone to wander from the truth, a small group should be committed to regular Bible study and should root any attempts at life change in careful application of the study. Bibles must be opened, read, studied, and learned from. It is impossible to overstate the importance of getting into the Word of God for discipleship.[31]

Consider just a few of the many Scriptures that point to the necessity of the Word of God.

- Hebrews 4:12: "The word of God is living and active, sharper than any two-edged sword, piercing to the division of soul and of spirit, of joints and of marrow, and discerning the thoughts and intentions of the heart" (ESV).

- Colossians 3:16: "Let the word of Christ dwell in you richly, teaching and admonishing one another in all wisdom, singing psalms and hymns and spiritual songs, with thankfulness in your hearts to God" (ESV).
- Luke 11:28: "[Jesus] said, 'Blessed rather are those who hear the word of God and keep it!' " (ESV).
- Matthew 4:4: "Man shall not live by bread alone, but by every word that comes from the mouth of God" (ESV).

Jesus himself clearly demonstrated the value of meditating on, memorizing, and metabolizing God's Word. When tempted in the wilderness by Satan, Jesus went straight to the Word to combat his enemy. Jesus had a firm command of the promises and prescriptions of God when he needed them the most. That's why we define our small groups as *biblical* relational environments. The Bible is vital to the disciple-making process.

2. The Importance of the Spirit of God

The power to change our lives does not come from us. I've seen churches that promote the dangerous idea that if we just grit our teeth and try harder to clean ourselves up, then all will be well. The "try harder" concept is something we can all fall into if we are not careful, but it eventually leads to a cycle of failure, guilt, and separation from God. The Spirit of God is the one who ultimately does the work of God in our lives. Second Corinthians 3:18 speaks about this transformation and reminds us where the power to change comes from: "We all, with unveiled face, beholding the glory of the Lord, are being transformed into the same image from one degree of glory to another. For this comes from the Lord who is the Spirit" (ESV). Jesus teaches us that if we are to bear spiritual fruit, we must abide in him. He tells us that apart from him we can do nothing, meaning nothing of eternal value.

We do have a hand in the transformation process. Christ invites us to remain in him as he is pruning us to be even more effective and bear more spiritual fruit. Our will and our decision-making capability clearly factor into the equation. The Bible calls us to cooperate with God as the Holy Spirit works in our lives. Second Peter 1:5–7 points to our responsibility when it says, "For this very reason, make every effort to supplement your faith with virtue, and virtue with knowledge, and knowledge with self-control, and self-control with steadfastness, and steadfastness with godliness, and godliness with brotherly affection, and brotherly affection with love" (ESV). Yet even though we are involved in the process, the power to change comes ultimately from the Holy Spirit. The Spirit of God does the work of transforming us. Romans 8:29 speaks of how we are "predestined to be conformed to the image of his Son" (ESV). Our growth in godliness is a miracle of God's grace, a spiritual act undertaken by a sovereign God.

This means that individuals as well as those who lead small groups must rely on the power of the Holy Spirit. We don't invite people to join a small group because we think we have something special to offer them. The power to change doesn't come from the group itself. But the group is a biblical relational environment used by God to be the means by which his Spirit brings lasting transformation to people's lives.

3. The Importance of the People of God

So how do people change? How do we grow as disciples of Jesus? What is it that changes us? It's the Word of God and the Spirit of God *working together with* the people of God. If you carefully study the Scriptures, you will find that almost every instruction in the Bible contains either a vertical directive or a horizontal directive. As Jesus said to his disciples, all of the Law and the Prophets can be summed up in the simple directive to love God and love others.

This means that we *cannot* separate relationships from the disciple-making process. Our interactions with other people are one of the means God uses to teach us truth. Relationships in the body of Christ are where we learn from others what a mature Christian life looks like. Some people encourage us and spur us on in our spiritual journey. Other people rub us the wrong way, and we must learn to be gracious and forgiving in our interactions with them.

We all need to experience the love of Christ in order to grow. The people of God demonstrating the love of God is the ultimate thing. Love is the ultimate sign of true discipleship (John 13:34–35). Learning to love others is a huge component of the disciple-making process. If we aren't intentionally striving to get along with other people, we are not growing in this area; we are not becoming spiritually mature, despite the amount of biblical information we may have acquired.

It's as simple as that.

For example, let's consider what Paul writes in Romans 12:9–21. Walk through this passage with me and take a moment to consider how many of the teachings in this passage apply to our interactions with other people.

- "Be devoted to one another in love."
- "Honor one another above yourselves."
- "Share with the Lord's people who are in need."
- "Practice hospitality."
- "Bless those who persecute you; bless and do not curse."
- "Rejoice with those who rejoice; mourn with those who mourn."
- "Live in harmony with one another."
- "Do not be proud, but be willing to associate with people of low position."
- "Do not be conceited."
- "Do not repay anyone evil for evil."
- "Be careful to do what is right in the eyes of everyone. If it is possible, as far as it depends on you, live at peace with everyone."
- "Do not take revenge, my dear friends, but leave room for God's wrath, for it is written: 'It is mine to avenge; I will repay,' says the Lord. On the contrary: 'If your enemy is hungry, feed him; if he is thirsty, give him something to drink. In doing this, you will heap burning coals on his head.'"

All of these instructions directly relate to our interactions with other people *in the church*. Growing as a disciple necessitates being involved in intentional relationships with other Christians on a consistent basis. God commands us to grow up in this way, because he knows how he created us! We are built with a relational need, and we can grow only as we engage in relationships with other believers. Failing to grow in this way leads to an unsatisfying form of Christianity, and unsatisfied Christians won't fight the spiritual fight as they should and are certainly not attractive to the lost. In order to be disciples who make disciples, we must be relationally connected with others.

One of my life verses is Hebrews 3:12–13: "See to it, brothers and sisters, that none of you has a sinful, unbelieving heart that turns away from the living God. But encourage one another daily, as long as it is called 'Today,' so that none of you may be hardened by sin's deceitfulness." In the original language, the word translated as "encourage" means to exhort or to admonish. It implies that we are to urge one another forward to godliness.

Look closely at the text again. According to the passage, how do I keep my heart from being hardened by sin's deceitfulness? Answer: through regular encouragement by the family of God. This encouragement can take a variety of forms. It might mean someone coming alongside me and saying, "Hey, well done. Keep up the good work." But it might be a friend challenging me to avoid temptation or resist a sinful pattern in my life, someone who in love says to me, "What in the world are you doing? Knock it off!" We need to be encouraged *and* challenged by others who will help us grow to maturity as followers of Christ.

Ask / Dr. Coleman

Why must a mature Christian love people? And how do you love someone you might not like?

That's a good distinction right there. We have to love people; we don't have to like them. God is love, and God loves even the unloving. He loves people when they do not love back; otherwise there would not have been hope for any of us. But you don't need to like everybody. I've got some people I don't like. But I have to love them.

I remember one student in seminary when I was teaching. He was a little cantankerous, didn't believe in the creation account of Genesis, and found fault with people who did. Nice boy, but it was kind of hard to like him. He was so proud of himself and how much he knew. I didn't argue with him, but we weren't on the same wavelength.

But you know, I committed to love that guy as Christ wanted me to love him. The student stayed with me and took another class. And before his seminary experience was over, that guy became one of the strongest believers and followers of Christ that we had.

I think of another man who was equally hard to like, when I was a pastor. He was an old horse-trader who lived just a mile from the church. He had five or six kids, and his house was dilapidated. I felt sorry for his wife.

I visited everybody in the community in those days—saint or sinner, it didn't matter to me. The first time I visited him, he told me he didn't have time for the church. When I visited him again, he said, "Well, preacher, I can't come to church because I don't know how to act, and my kids don't know how to act."

"That's no problem, sir," I said. "I'm used to any situation. I've preached out on the street. I can tolerate any kind of distraction. You bring those kids; they won't bother me."

He took me up on it. He came to church, and it was just like he said. Those kids were wild. They were hollering and screaming. I just kept on preaching. One of the members of the church came up to me, red in the face, and said, "Pastor, I don't know if

I can stand it anymore." But that man and his family came back, and the man got saved. I mean, he got saved! He cleaned up his house, he cleaned up those kids, and he and his family came to church all the time.

You have to love people until you can like them. The key is looking at people with the eyes of Jesus, because Jesus loves them. That's what I want in my life; the more that I can get that kind of love, the better I am. The better we all are.

Love is what constrains us to fulfill the Great Commission. It's not obedience. It's not a sense of duty. Duty gets brittle, and we can get weary in doing good. But love doesn't tire. Love doesn't grow weary. I'm thankful that one of the last things that Jesus reminded his disciples about was to love. The story is found in John 21. After the resurrection, some of the disciples had gone back to fishing. Jesus met them on the shore of the Sea of Galilee. They pulled their catch ashore, and Jesus invited them to join him for breakfast. After they ate, Jesus turned to Peter and said to the big fisherman, "Simon son of John, do you love me?" (John 21:15).

Isn't that interesting? Jesus didn't ask Peter, "Do you obey me?" He said, "Do you love me." Three times Jesus asked Peter that. On the third time, Peter was grieved that Jesus had spoken to him three times. (Many believe that it was because Peter earlier had denied his Lord three times.) But Jesus appealed to his love.

Peter knew he had blown it. He knew he had denied his Lord. But he knew, in that moment, that Jesus had forgiven him. Jesus wanted Peter to affirm that he loved him. That's the real issue. If you truly love God, you will fulfill all the rest. Isn't that the Law— to love God with all your heart, soul, strength, and mind, and to love your neighbor as yourself?

CASTING A VISION FOR RELATIONAL ENVIRONMENTS

At this point, you might agree that there is definitely a need for biblical relationships, but you also see a problem: your congregation has always done things differently. How do you change the way things have been done? How do cast this vision within your congregation, convincing them of their need for biblical relational environments?

One common challenge leaders face is that many church cultures have never experienced how helpful and necessary biblical relational environments are to the spiritual maturation process. People may know at a head level that Jesus made his disciples in the context of relationships, and we may even teach or preach this, but we fill our days with administrative tasks, creating and implementing programs in the church that have limited opportunities for relational interaction.

For instance, we might encourage our men's ministry to host regular cleanup days on which the men work together on the church grounds or out in the community. The cleanup work needs to be done, but we neglect the biblical and relational components of the ministry. Two men may spend the day working side by side, but they never talk honestly about their lives, nor is there any attempt to connect the work they are doing with their spiritual growth, with God's purposes. This needs to change.

Church leaders begin casting the vision for relational environments by being intentional in their own relationships. This can be as simple as regularly gathering together with other believers to study and apply the Bible, as we mentioned in the previous chapter. I ask pastors during our training seminars, "How many of you have at least one good friend?" Most of the pastors and church leaders will raise their hand. But then I'll begin to define what a good friend is in the context of Hebrews 3:12–13, someone you meet with regularly to exhort and admonish each other so your hearts aren't hardened through sin's deceitfulness. Then I ask, "How many of you have a friend like this?" Very few church leaders raise their hands. When I push further, they admit that their real friend is their wife or someone from college who lives in another state. And when I ask them why they don't have friends in their churches, they tell me that they are too busy or that people can't understand a pastor's life. They say that if they really share what they feel, people will be surprised and will lose respect for them. I find that the devil has pushed these pastors into an emotional corner where he can beat them up, scare them, and even entice them to sin—and they have no one with whom to share this struggle.

The truth that leaders often forget is that we *all* share common issues and struggles; no temptation has overtaken us but that which is common to man. We all need people in our lives with whom we can be real. Without them, we are an easy target for burnout, sin, loneliness, and a lack of effectiveness that leads to pride or shame. And even if a leader tries to deny this, his lack of transparency and accountability will have an effect on the rest of the church; as the head goes, the body follows.

This is a recipe for disaster. Because leaders have failed to correctly define biblical relationships and live in them, our churches are filled with people who have no understanding of what it means to be in a discipling relationship. We are not in biblical relationship with one another if all we do is sit next to each other on Sunday morning. We are not in biblical relationship if we go golfing and talk only about improving our game. We are not in biblical relationship if all we do is preach to people, even if we preach the truth. Preaching is a key part of the disciple-making process, but preaching alone will not make disciples. Jesus' example shows us that discipleship is the result of applying a relational methodology. Growing together with the people of God is vital to the process.

After pastors learn this truth for themselves and apply it in their own lives, they can begin to develop systems in which biblical relational environments are open and available to everyone in the church. It's the job of a church leader to both administrate biblical relationship and regularly communicate the need for biblical relational environments. A big part of a pastor's job as a vision caster is to train his congregation to see the need for and to desire discipleship in the first place. Because cultural patterns of independence and self-reliance are ingrained in us, few people truly want to be humble before God and obedient to him. Far fewer want to receive admonishment or correction from others, even if the other people are wiser than they are. Yet we teach people that the path of Christian maturity involves learning how to live in submission to others. To grow as a disciple, we must learn to invite others to speak wise counsel to us. Proverbs 20:18 says, "Plans are established by seeking advice." We need to teach people to value advice from others and to regularly seek it out.

Two key Scriptures point to the give-and-take nature of biblical relationships within the context of the church.

- *The first Scripture speaks to church leaders.* First Peter 5:2 says, "Be shepherds of God's flock that is under your care." This verse points to the pastor's responsibility to see that the people are being cared for spiritually. We do this by making sure that our people have the opportunity to be in a group led by someone who knows their name and cares for their spiritual well-being. The leaders of these groups are trained by the leadership of the church, and their job is to facilitate a group in such a way that people are learning the Word and growing as disciples of Jesus. Facilitation, as opposed to teaching, allows people to be more involved in learning and to interact with others. As people interact with each other, we learn where they are at in their spiritual growth.

- *The second Scripture refers to the people of God.* As a leader, I am often reminded of my responsibility to care for and serve God's people. But it is also true that every Christian has a responsibility as well — to obey and submit to the leadership of the church. Hebrews 13:17 says, "Obey your leaders and submit to them, for they are keeping watch over your souls, as those who will have to give an account. Let them do this with joy and not with groaning, for that would be of no advantage to you" (ESV). In other words, God puts leaders in the church for a reason — to keep an eye on the spiritual condition of the body. Disciples show that they are growing and maturing as they learn to joyfully follow the leaders of the church.

The relationship between a small group leader and a small group member can be illustrated by the coaching metaphor we talked about earlier. It's a coach's job to teach, train, and guide. People involved in a discipling relationship should expect their leader to speak into their life. They should value this input, because they have a biblical vision for growth and maturity. Those who are spiritually mature will want to hear from their shepherds and coaches, because they appreciate the wise counsel they offer. They will always test this counsel against the Word, but they will be humble enough to submit to their leaders and trust their guidance. This is a key part of the vision you need to impart to your church, helping people understand that when someone shares an honest word of challenge or encouragement, it is a good and gracious act of love. Instead of getting upset or offended, a mature believer will value and appreciate the courage shown in caring enough to share. Again, your church needs to grasp that a small group is more than just a social circle; it's a group that meets with a goal—to grow more and more into the likeness of Christ.

WORKING TOGETHER

When people are in biblical relationships with one another, growth and maturity is the result. People learn how to get along with each other. They come to see how their actions affect other people, and vice versa. They learn how to handle disappointment, how to go through loss, and how to celebrate as a team. Today across North America, there are large numbers of Christians who aren't in biblical relationships in which they're accountable to someone. Spiritually immature people attend church about half as often as they say they do, and when they do attend, they are often not meaningfully engaged in spiritual growth.[32] That's why we need to make this shift.

Jerry Harris is a friend who pastors a church called The Crossing, located in Quincy, Illinois, which we mentioned earlier in the book. We became close friends while working through several of the shifts we describe in this book. When we first met, Jerry was completely focused on reaching lost people—and he was very effective at it! But he sensed that the people he was reaching weren't growing and maturing, and he knew that the church needed to change. The thought of redesigning his entire church culture around the concepts we are talking about seemed overwhelming to him. We spent several fun-filled days together arguing about the basic principles underlying his philosophy of ministry. Jerry admitted that it was difficult for him to wrap his mind around the idea that discipleship was the core function of the church. Yet eventually he became convinced that this was indeed the way of Jesus and the focus of the Great Commission. He knew that shifts had to be made. So he took the first step. Over time, he successfully led his church to make a *discipleshift*—a change from a focus on seeking conversions to a focus on making disciples who make disciples. Jerry happens to lead a very large church—around five thousand in attendance over multiple locations. But the shifts he made, the changes we are talking about in this book, can be made regardless of the size of your church.

In the next chapter, we'll dig even deeper into the specific changes you need to make to shift from a program focus to a purposeful and intentional culture of discipleship. Now that we see the need for biblical relational environments in which people can grow together, we can get to the practical question: what do we actually equip the people in our churches to *do*?

The answer to that question can be as simple as doing what you already love to do, but taking it one step farther, adding the intentional purpose of discipleship to our everyday responsibilities, passions, and jobs.

KEY POINTS

- The true role of the church is to create biblical disciples *in relational environments.* Following Jesus and the apostles, we seek environments in which disciples are made not just through public gatherings but especially from house to house.
- There are three components needed to change a person's life—the Word of God, the Spirit of God, and the people of God. These three components work together to bring about spiritual maturity in people's lives.
- Church leaders begin to cast the vision for the need for relational environments by first being intentional in their own relationships. Leaders

must regularly gather together with other believers to study and apply the Bible and be honest about doing life together.

- Leaders of a church need to create systems in which biblical relationships are available to everyone in the church. It's the job of a church leader to both administrate biblical relationship (to set up the systems and correct the issues that spring from getting people together) and regularly communicate the need for biblical relational environments.

- A big part of a pastor's job as a vision caster is to train his congregation to see the need for and to desire discipleship in the first place. Few people truly want to be humble before God and obedient to him. Far fewer want to receive admonishment or correction from others.

- Remember that there are three people required to work in the process. The disciple maker, the one who is being discipled, and God. I cannot do God's part, and I cannot do the disciple's part; I can only do mine. My job as a leader is to make opportunities available, but I cannot make someone get involved. I can feel good about what I am doing if I have done my best (by God's strength and direction) to do my part in my own growth and in the growth of others.

Chapter 8

ROLLING UP OUR SLEEVES
AND ENGAGING

What do you actually equip people in the church to do?

When Bobby Harrington first planted Harpeth Community Church (near the Harpeth River) in the greater Nashville, Tennessee, area, he panicked. It was hard enough taking the plunge and leaving the security of an established church to become a church planter. Now he was faced with the reality of the mission. How would he ever reach his community for Jesus?[33]

Bobby fasted, prayed, and worked out an action plan. In addition to developing relationships with unchurched people in different contexts, he developed a unique focus to his efforts. He was a Canadian, and both he and his son loved playing hockey, and they knew that there were few committed Christians in the community hockey leagues they were part of in the Franklin-Nashville area. So they decided that instead of simply attending the practices and games and occasionally talking to a few people at the rink, they would purposefully and intentionally enter the world of hockey and build significant friendships with the players and their families.

Bobby signed on to coach a couple of teams. His son, a capable hockey player and a committed young Christian, joined his dad in the mission. They dedicated time to hanging out with the boys and their families, traveling with them to games in nearby cities, joking together, and soon they became close friends with many of the players and their dads. Since there were now established relationships, it was a natural and simple next step for Bobby and his son to invite these families to their new church.

Many of the hockey families ended up visiting the church, and in the second year of his coaching, more than half of the families on the team became regular attendees. Bobby would often ask them to serve at the church in all kinds of ways, even though they weren't yet Christians. He introduced them to the teachings of the Bible and gave them space and time to process the claims of the gospel. Many became Christians, and in the early days, their church became known as the "hockey church."

In this chapter, we want to take a closer look at the way we equip disciples to enter the world for the sake of the gospel and lead people through the stages of discipleship. We want churches to make the shift from program to purpose, from activities that just draw crowds or impart information to activities that take place in relational environments where discipleship occurs.

THE METHODOLOGY EXPLAINED

If our methodology is based on the method Jesus used to make disciples, we can find answers by asking ourselves three questions.

1. What did Jesus do?
2. How do I replicate his method in my own life as a church leader?
3. What do I teach others to do?

Methods continually change as we exegete the culture. Circumstances will change as well. This is why every church will look different, even if they all share the same convictions and basic theology. Though this book is written out of an American context, there are certainly differences we have not considered based on regional cultures. Those details cannot be ignored. What worked for one church in the South may not work in the Midwest. Some who live in the city may try to use methods that succeeded in a rural area and fail because they didn't begin with basic biblical principles. These principles are true in every situation and for every age, regardless of where we live or the size of our church. The application of these principles, however, will vary based on our location and context. Let's look at the core biblical principles that underlie what Jesus did to make disciples who make disciples.

If we study Jesus' method for making disciples and then study how the early church repeated this pattern, we discern a blueprint that we can follow as well. Many of the churches in the Relational Discipleship Network use this simple blueprint, based on four words.

Share
Connect
Minister
Disciple

Jesus *shared* who he was through words and deeds. When people accepted his message, he invited then to *connect* with him in relationship. During that time of sharing life together, he taught them the truth about himself. As these disciples grew, Jesus trained them to *minister* to the lost and to his other followers. Finally, after Jesus rose from the dead, he deployed his followers to *disciple* others.

We call this the SCMD methodology: Share, Connect, Minister, and Disciple.

The early church followed the same pattern. On the day of Pentecost, Peter preached to three thousand people. Those people then began to connect in the temple courts and from house to house with those who were baptized (Acts 2:42–46). As people grew, they were deployed to service; for example, the seven deacons were chosen to care for the Greek widows (Acts 6). When persecution hit the church in Jerusalem, Philip went to Samaria and made disciples there (Acts 8). Paul and the rest of the disciples repeated the process wherever they went, and those they discipled repeated that same process, and so on (2 Tim. 2:2).

As his disciples today, we *share* our lives with other people, eventually also sharing the gospel — the good news about Jesus and what he has done for us and can do for them. We then *connect* with those who accept this message and help them connect with Christ and other believers in relationship through his church. Next, we help these new disciples take steps to grow, by supplying a place for them to learn how to *minister* in Jesus' name. And finally, when they are ready, we deploy them, releasing them to *disciple* other people in the same way. The "Five Stages of Discipleship" diagram from chapter 3 shows how these four activities align with the various stages of growth for a maturing disciple.

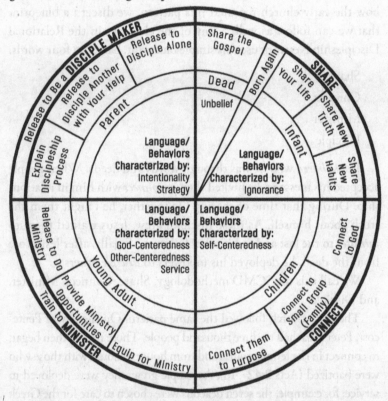

Whenever we release someone to be a disciple maker, we want them to understand the process. If you look at the outer circle of the diagram, you'll find the words *Share*, *Connect*, *Minister*, and *Disciple*. Observe how each of these activities corresponds to a different stage of growth and maturity. We share our lives and the gospel with people who are spiritually dead and with infants in the faith. When they are at the child stage, we help them grow by connecting them to God, to groups of other believers, and to God's purposes for their life as a disciple. Next, we seek to equip them for ministry as they grow into spiritual young adults. We help them figure out their gifts and calling. We help them find a place to use their gifts with good coaching. Finally, when they reach the mature adult stage (no one is ever completely mature), we release them to minister and make disciples.

Dr. Robert Coleman, a coauthor of this book, presented a similar pattern fifty years ago in his book *The Master Plan of Evangelism*. Dr. Coleman uses nine words to describe these same stages. We've taken his nine-word description of this process and overlaid it onto our four-word strategy. Why? Because we believe that seeing how these grids fit together offers a fuller, more complete picture of what we are talking about in the disciple-making process.

Again, we start with our question: what does a leader actually equip people in the church to do? We equip people to understand and follow Jesus' method of discipleship. We seek to guide disciples as Jesus guided disciples. As you will now see, his method involves four natural developmental stages.

1. Share

In the first stage, we *incarnate* Christ's life in a lost world and then *invite* people to respond to Christ.

The Bible teaches us that love is the hallmark of people who truly know Jesus (John 13:35; Eph. 5:1–2). Discipleship begins with a desire and commitment to share this love. Robert Coleman's teaching helps us make the Share phase very specific: as we follow Jesus' method, we emulate the incarnation of Jesus as we enter into the lost and hurting world, and then, in the process, we give an invitation for people to respond to Jesus through us.

Incarnation means that, like Jesus, we enter into a lost world as ministers. God became "incarnate" in our world in the person of Jesus (John 1). Love for God and love for lost people inspired Jesus. He was sent into the world (John 3:16) to seek and save the lost (Luke 19:10). When we seek to truly follow Jesus, we will do what he did. We will look at our world — our neighbors, relatives, and coworkers — and ask, "How does God want me to enter into the lives of these people and show them his love?"

Without Jesus, people have lost their way. There are only two kinds of people—not black and white or Democrat and Republican or American and not or rich and poor. There are only those who are saved and those who are not saved. People without Jesus may be full of the world, but they are missing life's true meaning. They may be hungry, sad, in despair, addicted to harmful substances, and wandering aimlessly. Some may not have hit bottom. They may not see their need for Jesus or even desire him at all.

Loving relationships are the bridge to communicate the gospel and begin the discipleship process. Relationships create a bridge over which the Word of God can travel and be heard and received. Our love is the context in which the Spirit of God uses the Word of God to bring conviction. We see that Jesus entered into people's lives and built relationships with them at their point of need. After touching on their need, he would point his listeners to God's kingdom. Likewise, we look for appropriate ways to meet needs and for opportunities to point people to the reality of God's salvation and his kingdom.

The work of reaching a lost world begins with our primary relationships in life—the people in our neighborhood, the people we work with, the people we spend time with day after day. God may have placed certain individuals in your life right now where you can naturally invest in a relationship. God loves them; you can show them his love by your actions.

The second way we can reach the lost is through the ministries of the church. Churches can reach out corporately through small groups, community groups, church services, and various ministries. We can find incarnational ways to reach out as a church by meeting people's needs and pointing them to Jesus. As in our individual friendships, we should intentionally build bridges to people by sharing God's love, helping them with their needs, and then, in the process, inviting them to consider following Jesus with us as a church family.

Invitation means that, like Jesus, we should invite people to respond to him. Jesus was constantly praying and asking God to lead him. As Jesus ministered to a lost world, he found people who were responsive to his call. "Follow me," Jesus would say. He made even greater investments of his time and energy into those who were responsive to his message. He chose to focus on the few, not the many.

In our churches today, we too need to focus on those who are responsive, those who demonstrate spiritual hunger and a desire to grow. As we build relational bridges to people, and as we pray and ask God to open doors, we will see God bring people to us. We want to "go with the goers." This doesn't mean ignoring those who don't take responsive steps. On the contrary, we keep on loving them, and we keep hoping that someday they will be ready to cross over that bridge. As a pastor, I've seen people come to church year after year, never taking a step to grow or change, until finally God orchestrated the right circumstances to bring them to their knees. Today they are living out his calling as disciples of Jesus who make disciples.

The Engel Scale is a popular model that can be used to help people better understand the idea that conversion is a process, not a one-time event.[34] As the scale indicates, a conversion to Christ is not the first moment in this process. It is typically preceded by "mini-decisions" or "small steps" that lead up to the decision to surrender to Christ. Reading the scale from the bottom up, notice how people process their faith and grow into a commitment as God leads them.

+5	Stewardship
+4	Communion with God
+3	Conceptual and behavioral growth
+2	Incorporation into body
+1	Post-decision evaluation
	New birth
-1	Repentance and faith in Christ
-2	Decision to act
-3	Personal problem recognition
-4	Positive attitude towards gospel
-5	Grasp implications of gospel
-6	Awareness of fundamentals of gospel
-7	Initial awareness of gospel
-8	Awareness of supreme being, no knowledge of gospel

The Engel Scale

Disciple makers learn that discipling lost people is a process. (Note that we like to describe it as discipling lost people, not evangelism.) If someone starts the faith journey at −8, it is unwise to try to move them all the way to −1, the point of repentance and faith in Christ, after one interaction. They will likely respond negatively. Instead we must give them time and space to process the claims of Christ, by helping them move one step at a time, from −8 to −7, then from −7 to −6, and so forth. The key in this is to look for receptivity, engagement, and direction. Like Jesus, we want to look for people whom God is drawing to himself through us. And like Jesus, we want to lead responsive individuals to the next level by getting them connected with other disciples.

When people are receptive to Jesus and the message of the gospel, they are ready to be born again (John 3:5; Titus 3:4−7). They will show this by asking for Christ's forgiveness, relying on his sacrifice and the Holy Spirit, and by committing themselves to become his disciples (Acts 2:36−42). They are then transferred from the kingdom of spiritual death into the kingdom of light (Col. 1:13−14). They are now spiritual infants who need to connect with spiritual parents for discipleship.

2. Connect

In the second stage, we help new Christians *associate* with other disciples and *consecrate* themselves to God.

The Bible does not envision solo or isolated Christians. Following Jesus is something we can do effectively only if we are connected to other disciples. It takes a community. That is why the local church has always been God's primary environment for making them. Robert Coleman's research on Jesus' method shows us that at this stage, we should take receptive people and connect them with other disciples through regular association and consecration, teaching them to obey the teachings of Jesus.

Association means that, like Jesus, we establish ongoing relational connections with those who respond to him. Jesus stayed with people whom God had raised up and who were responsive to his call. He shows us that we have to be close to people to build discipling relationships like Jesus did. Jesus concentrated on and developed closer relationships with the few learners who were drawn to him. They walked the trails together. They went to the synagogue together. They went up to the mountains and spent time away from the pressures of regular work. These learners watched what Jesus was doing, and he helped them internalize his beliefs, practices, and emotions.

For most of us, small groups will provide the most common foundational context for these connections to occur in the local church. As people get connected to God and to each other in a small group, the discipleship process can blossom. Sometimes the key connections will be in the more intimate discipling groups of two to four men or women in same-gender groups.

Consecration **means that, like Jesus, we help people to obey God's teachings.** The invitation Jesus gave to his disciples, even at the earliest stage, was not to just "accept Christ" or simply believe what Jesus was teaching. It was an invitation to "follow me." As discussed above, discipleship meant "do what I do; go where I go." Today we often need to refer to this as the difference between cultural Christians and biblical disciples. So many people have not been taught the importance of following what Jesus teaches, and even if they have, there is little modeling to show them how, and there is little accountability through relationships to support life change.

Obedience is a word few people like to hear today, but obedience to Christ is the means by which we grow to be like Jesus. Making disciples is about teaching people to obey everything that Jesus taught and commanded (Matt. 28:19–20). Again, this type of teaching can happen through sermons, but most often it happens in small groups. This is where we get into the nitty-gritty details of struggles and difficulties we might have in following a particular teaching or obeying in a specific area of our life. The goal of teaching in the context of the Great Commission is to replace what people have heard from the world with what Jesus has said, emphasizing the practical aspects of being a disciple.

As we keep saying, Scripture is essential in this part of the process. The Bible says that faith comes from hearing God's Word

(Rom. 10:17). God says that his Word will "not return to me empty, but will accomplish what I desire and achieve the purpose for which I sent it" (Isa. 55:11). If we want to follow Jesus and obey all that he has taught us, we must first know and understand what he teaches.

3. Train to Minister

In the third stage, we *demonstrate* service to others, *delegate* service opportunities, and *supervise* the progress.

Once a Christian has become relationally connected with other disciples and is learning how to obey Christ, he or she will begin to experience spiritual growth. This will lead to a growing interest in serving others, using the gifts, skills, wisdom, and abilities that God has given him or her to honor God and bless others. As Robert Coleman shows us, this stage of discipleship focuses on demonstration (Jesus first set the example), then delegation (Jesus gave ministry work to his disciples), and then supervision (Jesus checked up on them, and debriefed and coached them).

Demonstration means that Jesus showed his disciples how to minister. Jesus connected with his disciples and let them see his priorities and values lived out in everyday life. He shared the inner life of his soul with them. He cared for people. He spoke to people to whom nobody else would. He healed people who desperately needed healing. He read Scriptures and explained them to people. His disciples could see his compassion. They watched, listened, and then tried to emulate Jesus. When they wanted to learn how to pray, Jesus didn't give them a book to read on prayer or a lecture on prayer. He gave them a demonstration. He prayed.

When it comes to learning how to minister, demonstration is what people are looking for. They want to be shown *how* if they are going to be expected to serve. As disciple makers, we must let them see what's important. Along with your successes, they'll need to see your shortcomings and failures, how you handle the mistakes you make. Don't be afraid to acknowledge these as well. Every sincere believer fails and turns again to the grace of God, resting on the fact that Jesus has paid the price for his sin. He rests in Christ and in the love of God and is renewed and motivated to try again. Every new believer needs to know that it's okay to share their failings, that this is a key part of the growth process. If you model this to them, they will begin to see the pattern of transformation, motivated by the good news of God's grace.

Delegation simply means that Jesus gave his disciples something to do. You delegate when you assign someone a task. Jesus gave his disciples specific ministry tasks to accomplish. For instance, just before the feeding of the five thousand, Jesus saw a large crowd approaching. He asked Philip, "Where are we to buy bread, so that these people may eat?" (John 6:5 ESV). Jesus was merely testing Philip, because he already knew what he was going to do. He then delegated to his disciples the task of gathering people into groups and then the distribution of the bread. Jesus gave specific assignments to them, using their gifts and skills to prepare them for future leadership roles.

The same is true for disciple makers today. Delegation means we not only encourage people to do ministry in Jesus' name but also _supply opportunities and places_ for them to do ministry. We give people a sense that they have a kingdom purpose. People learn best by doing, and disciple makers need to give people a time and place when and where they can participate in doing something, or they will soon get bored and walk away. I find it ironic that many men who lead in the workplace or out in the world end up doing little to promote the mission of the church. Men tend to be motivated by opportunities to act and do, and if the church fails to provide opportunities for these men to work and lead, they will take their time and skills elsewhere. When you win the men, you win the families.

Supervision means that Jesus made his disciples accountable. Supervision (sometimes called coaching) is tremendously important to the discipleship process. Many churches are able to connect people and get them involved in serving, but then they never follow up with the people to find out how they're doing. They recruit and direct, but they don't work with people to hone their abilities or overcome their weaknesses so they can become more focused and effective. Jesus did more than sharing and connecting; he trained his disciples by having times of review with them. He asked them questions. He confronted negative attitudes and character traits. He affirmed their strengths and reinforced their identity in God.

Again, many churches push the right emphasis of serving, but the serving is never supervised. Church leaders may say, "Okay, you've become a Christian. Now you need to go out and serve. But the poor, confused Christian is left scratching his head, thinking, *Okay, but where do I do that? How do I do that? Where do I start? What does that look like?* Disciple-making churches not only model service, teach it, and involve people in it; they also provide ongoing supervision. They ask good questions, providing positive but constructive feedback. They help people to be practically effective in ministry.

4. Release to Be a Disciple Maker

In the final stage, we expect mature disciples to learn to *reproduce* other disciples, and we trust the Holy Spirit's *impartation* in their lives to guide them.

Once a Christian has grown into a spiritual young adult, they will naturally minister to others, because their heart is growing and changing. They are now possessed by a genuine love for God and for his kingdom, and they understand the need for the ministries of the church. At this stage, young adults are not intentional; they love God and love others but have not yet made the jump to serving with the purpose of making disciples of others.

The Bible points out that no one can be mature without experiencing the love of God in Christ and loving others in turn. It is difficult to envision someone who has been truly saved by Jesus and truly loves lost people but does nothing to help people come to Christ, and be all that he or she can be. It is hard to see those who avoid involvement in spiritual parenting as having mature biblical love.

At a practical level, can we say that a parent is spiritually mature if they do not disciple their children in obedience to God's Word (Deut. 6:6–9; Eph. 6:4)? Part of the reason why we have trouble answering these questions lies in our definition of discipleship. In one sense, we can say that each of us is always involved in making disciples by the way we live our lives. We have a natural influence in the lives of others. (Everyone influences someone.) In this sense, any

Christian is contributing to discipling others if they regularly attend church, tithe, and serve, because they are helping the church disciple others. But the question still stands: must we *personally* disciple others to be considered mature in Christ?

It is difficult for me to say that someone is truly mature in Christ if he or she does not personally obey Jesus' teaching to make disciples, as stated in the Great Commission (Matt. 28:19–20). Can we truly be *like Christ*, who personally made disciples, and not personally make disciples ourselves? Jesus taught his disciples to personally make disciples. His last words to them were very clear. They had a mission from him to do exactly that. So the answer to all of these questions is yes. A mature disciple is a person who makes other disciples who are released to *disciple* others. Robert Coleman shows us that the culmination of the discipleship process must necessarily involve these two additional and related aspects: *reproduction* and *impartation* (the presence of the Holy Spirit).

Reproduction means that Jesus anticipated fruitfulness. Jesus instilled a vision for multiplication in his disciples. He painted a picture of the kingdom as a place of growth and multiplication, and he dreamed with them about their role in the harvest to come. He expected that his disciples would grow spiritually and eventually become spiritual shepherds and parents who reproduced other disciples who, in turn, would eventually become spiritual parents.

This is why the biblical teaching on the ministry of all believers and the coaching role of leaders is so important to emphasize (Eph. 4:11–13; Rom. 12:3–8). *Every* disciple has the capability and the responsibility to minister to others in God's name. We are all ambassadors, lights in the world, ministers of reconciliation. Understood this way, it's clear that it is the role of every believer to grow up to be a minister and to make disciples, and it is the role of every minister, pastor, and elder to train, equip, and coach every disciple to become a minister who makes disciples.

Impartation means that Jesus gave his followers his Spirit. Jesus doesn't *send* us anywhere. He *goes* with us wherever we are. Better said, we are to seek to go with him wherever he is. God's work can be done only in his power and at his direction. Jesus said that if we abide in him, we will bear much fruit. Jesus wasn't releasing his disciples into the world without him. He promised them that he was going to be in relationship with them forever. He didn't leave them as orphans. He left them the Holy Spirit.

Sometimes people will be in relationship with us; we'll raise them up and then we separate to begin the process with others. This does not mean that we are not in relationship anymore; it merely means that the nature of our relationship has changed. We never graduate from the need for relationship, so now we become colaborers who get together for encouragement and accountability. Meanwhile, we begin the process of discipling the new person God leads us to. Bobby and Cindy Harrington raised their daughter Ashley to be a minister of Christ and a disciple maker. Ashley is a young lady who loves the Lord and seeks to serve him and make others his disciples. When she left home to attend a university, Ashley worked at a Sonic Drive-In restaurant to make some extra money. As she developed relationships with her coworkers, she learned that some of them were very far from God and did not know anything about Jesus. So Ashley started a Bible study and invited these folks to join her. Every week they met, studied the Bible, and built relationships. It wasn't long before one of the young men became a Christian. Bobby and Cindy's daughter is now a mature disciple, a co-minister serving Christ alongside Bobby and his wife. They still have relationship (obviously), but now there is another disciple maker reaching the world for Jesus one person at a time.

The best indicator that someone is mature is *not* that they are making disciples but that they are making disciples who have gone on to be disciple makers themselves. A mature disciple maker can point to several people whom he has discipled who are now discipling others. Growing into the final stage of maturity as a disciple means that we release people from being actively discipled by us, but again we don't release them from relationship. We continue to work and serve together as co-laborers for the cause of Christ. The reason I feel led to say this over and over again is because so many Christians who believe they are disciple makers have no real relationships in their lives. It is true that I believe relationship is the best way to make disciples, but I also believe that real relationship is the result of having been truly discipled. A mature spiritual person is relational. Relationship is not just a means to an end but also the end itself— one who is in relationship with God and others.

KEY POINTS

- Jesus did indeed have a strategy for drawing people closer to God. His main focus was investing in a small group of people so that they, in turn, would grow to spiritual maturity and make more disciples.
- As we study Jesus' methodology for disciple making, four important questions come to mind: (1) What did Jesus do? (2) What do I do now in my own life as a church leader? (3) What do I teach others to do? (4) What does real teaching look like (it's not just a transfer of information)?
- Jesus *shared* with people who he was through words and deeds. When people accepted his message, he invited them to *connect* with him in relationship. During that time of sharing life together, he taught them the truth about God. As these disciples grew, Jesus trained them to *minister* to the lost and to his other followers. Finally, after he rose from the dead, he deployed his followers to *disciple* others.
- We've named Jesus' methodology Share, Connect, Minister, and Disciple, or SCMD. For us in this day and age, it means that we *share* our lives with people. As we do, we share the gospel with them. Those who accept the message, we *connect* with, and as we do, we help them connect with Christ and with other believers. As we do life with these new disciples, we help supply a place for them to learn how to *minister* in Jesus' name. Finally, when they are ready, we release them to *disciple* others.

SHIFT

4

From Activity
to Relationship

Chapter 9

RETHINKING OUR PRACTICES

How does each ministry in your church lead to discipleship?

A colleague of ours is the senior pastor of an established medium-sized church. He told us about three different—yet strangely very similar—conversations he had in the church lobby after a recent Sunday morning worship service.

The first was with a man named Edward, a retiree who once worked as a choir director at a nearby university. Edward told his pastor that he saw the need for more special music in the service. He envisioned a men's quartet that would develop a repertoire of inspirational special numbers and perform once a month, perhaps also traveling to rest homes, prisons, and special functions around the county. Edward recognized that the church's worship services were blended, involving both traditional and contemporary music, so he also wanted to enlist the help of the musicians on the church's worship team. He sought permission to hold open tryouts for his men's quartet, and he wanted to put a notice in the bulletin soon, as well as announce the tryouts from the pulpit next Sunday.

The second conversation was with Rosalie, a mother of two teenage daughters. Rosalie's heart was solidly behind the women's ministries program, she said. She quoted Titus 2:4 about older women training up the younger women and lamented about how she wasn't seeing that happen in the church as much as it should. She envisioned a monthly women's praise gathering to supplement the existing

169

women's weekly Bible studies. At this monthly gathering, women of all ages could gather for a time of teaching and worship, as well as foster intergenerational relationships. She was willing and eager to work with the women's ministries coordinator to start the program and help run it. All she needed was the green light from the pastor.

The third conversation was with Butch, a first-year student at community college. Butch loved baseball and girls, he announced, so he wanted to see the church start a coed softball team so the young singles of the church could mix and mingle and play other teams from around the city. A league was being formed, and a number of other churches in the area were starting teams. Butch thought it was a great idea and would really boost the spirit of the college-age students. He offered to head up the team.

Three conversations. One Sunday morning. All three people well-meaning Christians who want to start ministries at the church. Something good is happening in the church, because people are coming to believe that ministry is for them. But this alone can still lead to a problem. If you were in the pastor's shoes, what would you have done? How would you have answered Edward, Rosalie, and Butch?

THE NECESSITY OF ALIGNMENT

Stories such as these happen regularly in any church. Good people want to do a whole bunch of good things, and if a church isn't careful, it's easy to start up a smorgasbord of ministries and go a hundred different directions at once.

We believe in the priesthood of every believer, and we want to get people into the game. Yet there is only so much energy and so many resources in your church, and you must use them for the most important things. You can end up doing a lot of things not very well and become a mile wide and an inch deep. You must direct your people to things that make the biggest impact. There is also a difference between what you allow and encourage people to do organically (on their own time) and what you back with your church's time, energy, and resources. Problems arise anytime a church doesn't think through this intentionally and strategically. So to counteract this trend, it's important for leaders to cast a vision for why the church does what it does, and then stick to that vision.

The fourth shift we advocate closely follows the last shift — from programs to purpose. It's a shift from activity to relationship. Though we have already spent time emphasizing the importance of relationships in fulfilling the church's mission to make disciples, this fourth shift sheds additional light on the role of various ministries in a church and the way the church is organized to support and strengthen these ministries. We believe that instead of busying itself with well-intentioned yet haphazardly focused activities, a church should make an intentional shift that nurtures the type of biblical relational discipleship we have been talking about. Since making disciples is the main reason why a church exists, everything in the corporate body of the local church needs to be aligned in a way that funnels people toward these discipleship environments, the most notable of which is the relational small group.

Within this shift, we are advocating the principle of *alignment*, in which every program and ministry of a church exists in harmony with the overall goal of making disciples. Various ministries are no longer seen as isolated components of the church. They are not silos functioning as competitors for resources and leaders. If a program is to exist (and clearly some should), it must move people to venues where spiritual growth can occur. Everything the church does relates in some way to the primary mission of discipleship. By applying this principle, church leaders protect their people from spending energy on things that lead to something other than what Jesus would consider success. Success for the church isn't feeding the poor a meal to satisfy their hunger. Success is feeding the poor in such a way that they will wonder why we are doing what we do. Our actions should lead them to hunger for the Bread of Life.

Let's examine the problem of misalignment, with an eye to finding a solution. We've discovered that in most churches today, the ministries aren't aligned with any overarching sense of purpose. Anytime I ask pastors about the ministries in their churches, they almost always speak about them in isolated, unattached terms, saying things like, "We've got a great men's group," or "Our youth pastor is really dynamic," or "Every other Saturday, a bunch of us go down to the homeless mission and volunteer." If you press a pastor further, he might say things like, "Well, all our ministries are about glorifying God," or "We want our people to grow in the faith," or "Our church has a long-standing tradition of providing lots of opportunities for our people to get involved." But the focus is seldom as clear as it could be.

The reality is that many ministries within a church exist without any clear, overall sense of purpose. They operate in isolation and don't end up reproducing people who are committed to the Lord and know how to make disciples. The ministries were started because good people wanted them. Year after year they continue, even if there's no great reason for them any longer, because they have become sacred over time and nobody wants to challenge their existence, much less kill them off if they're ineffective.

Judging effectiveness can be very subjective. If a person values people getting together to play softball, then the social aspect of the ministry is what makes it effective in their minds. It meets a felt need in people. But we need to ask another question as well: is this program effective as Jesus defines effectiveness? Hanging out and having fun is important, but if the program's purpose stops there, did we miss something vastly more important? Did we take energy that could have been better spent on fulfilling the God-given purpose of the church and waste it? Could we have made a change that led that fun social event to a much bigger kingdom win?

Ask yourself, What happens in a church if a program functions without any tie to discipleship? If we dig down deep, we find that the program exists only for itself. We found that we were hosting a junior high breakfast fundraiser every Mother's Day simply because the church had always hosted a junior high breakfast fundraiser on Mother's Day. The fundraiser continued not because there was any need to raise the funds but because it was a tradition in the church. We would spend time and energy recruiting people to run the fundraiser, come to the fundraiser, and give to the fundraiser. But we failed to ask the most important question of all: why are we having this fundraiser? How does this fundraiser contribute to the church's overall purpose of making disciples? What could we have been doing with this time and energy that would have made an eternal difference in the lives of our kids, their parents, and the world we live in?

Having a lot of unconnected programs in a church not only raises the question of effectiveness; it also creates a quality problem. The more programs you have and the more they are disconnected from a common purpose, the harder it is to lead, organize, and do things that really matter. It's far easier to do fewer things well than to do a lot of things haphazardly. Having a lot of unconnected ministries creates energy and staffing problems. A church has only so many human resources — both paid and volunteer — and having too many programs dilutes the mix of competent leadership.

It also becomes hard to sustain a large number of programs over the long haul. The original leaders get tired and drop out, so new staff or volunteers must be recruited. The people coming to the programs and participating get tired too. People get overwhelmed with the number of activities they engage in. The whole process becomes hard to reproduce season after season.

To summarize, the principle of alignment means that

- every program must be evaluated to see if it is really producing what Jesus values;
- every program that has the potential to make disciples, but isn't doing so, must align itself with the overall goal of biblical relational discipleship;
- we do fewer things in the church, and we do them well.

For new church planters and pastors, it's easier to have this discussion before you start a program and then decide not to do it than to have to kill a program that is loved by some of your influential people.

One good exercise is to have your church's leadership think through every program in your church, with an eye to discipleship.[35] For instance, your church might hold an Easter egg hunt each year. Ask: What's the purpose of the hunt? Who's the audience you're shooting for? What's the next step for people to take once they come to the hunt?

Ideally, with an Easter egg hunt, you want to create a fun environment to which your people can invite non-Christians so they can gain a different perspective of church. You want it to be easy for your people to invite their friends to a worship service after the hunt, because they now have a new understanding of what the people in the church look like and act like. Once your people's friends are at a service, you want them to hear about Jesus in a compelling way so they ask the ones who brought them more about some of the perceptions they have had. You want to have the believers you teach in your church to be ready for those questions and to know how to answer them or how to get answers for them. Eventually you want to move people to small groups, and so on. Each ministry and its leaders must be aligned to the overall purpose, and whatever you do needs to move people to the next stage. Every ministry in the church must funnel people back to the relational small group, where biblical discipleship can happen.

The challenge with alignment is that we as leaders are telling people to use the gifts they have been given for God's glory and his mission to reach the world. At the same time, if this is happening well, so many people will have what they think are good ideas about how to use those gifts. They want us to champion their causes, and to be honest, we love them and don't want to dissuade them from doing what is in part the right thing to do.

However, if we don't align people, ensuring that each and every ministry is matched and fitted to the purpose of making disciples, the real mission of the church, we will end up with a mismatched, disconnected community of people pursuing their own goals and programs that take on a life of their own. This is why every program in a church must be aligned with the goal of relational discipleship in view. We must learn to discern the difference between the good and the great, the well-meaning and the highly focused, the ineffective and the effective. Church leaders must examine every program and ask, What's the best use of our time according to the mission God has given us?

Ask/Dr. Coleman

Discuss the alignment concept. Why must everything in a church lead to discipleship?

If your church has a baseball team, for instance, the purpose of that baseball team is not just to play ball; it's to disciple people. In order to take people where you want to lead them, you have to start where they are. So baseball becomes a point of contact. A baseball team is a wonderful way of developing a relationship of trust that then brings the opportunity to present the gospel to people who will believe.

It could be a thousand other things besides baseball. A point of contact is developed wherever the people are and are interested. If you can identify that point of contact, then you have a place to begin. You have to teach from where the person is, to lead them where you want them to go. If you start at the point where you want them to go, often you lose them, because they're not ready to understand it yet.

Sometimes a person is prepared even before we realize it. You can proclaim that Jesus is Lord to people who might not recognize what that means. Still, in their hearts there is already a yearning to know that Someone is over all and sovereign.

PERMISSION TO SAY NO

I recognize that aligning all the programs in your church is easier said than done. As you work through this process of alignment, it's important to ask, How do all of our ministries work together using *similar language and structure* so that the ministries are not competing with one another? Recall what happened to the Tower of Babel when the language of the people building it was confused. A house divided against itself cannot stand, so a key part of aligning the ministries of your church is developing a common language — a playbook that everyone uses.

Alignment becomes particularly difficult if your church has been established for any significant length of time (which in most churches is about two years). For instance, at a friend's church, there was a strong contingent of people who believed that the church needed to serve the poor. They were all strong believers and had a number of Bible verses to back up their belief — and I'd agree with them: the church does have a responsibility to help people in need. In the same city, there was a parachurch ministry devoted to helping the poor. This ministry worked with single mothers and low-income families and people without homes. The contingent believed that the church should partner with the parachurch ministry, so church leaders met with leaders from this parachurch ministry to discuss various ways the church and the ministry might partner together.

But after talking about their goals and purpose, they were unable to find alignment. The church was committed to being a disciple-making church. When church leaders asked the leaders of the ministry what plan they had for making disciples, the ministry leaders indicated that their sole focus was to feed people and share the gospel with them. What would happen next? To that question, the ministry had no answer. When church leaders asked if they could help them develop a strategy for discipling people toward spiritual maturity, the parachurch ministry leaders declined. They said they were just overwhelmed with need, and while they believed discipleship was a good idea, all they really needed was volunteers. At the end of the day, this church and parachurch ministry could not align on a common mission.

Though the church leaders were prepared to assist the parachurch ministry in the discipleship process, they felt that without that shared goal, getting involved with this project would have been a good thing but not a great thing. The church had made a deliberate decision to focus all their energies and efforts on making disciples, and now they faced a choice. Would they commit resources to something that was not part of that core mission? Unfortunately, their decision did not sit well with the contingent, who believed that the church had a biblical mandate to help the poor. Tension and conflict erupted, and a number of families and individuals left the church. It was a hard decision for the leaders, but one they felt was necessary to stay focused and aligned in order to accomplish what God was calling them to do.

This illustrates why alignment is one of the hardest things churches grapple with. To say yes to your calling, you must necessarily say no to a lot of good things, and when you say no to a lot of good things, you say no to a lot of good people who don't understand why you're saying no. You're saying no to something they are emotionally invested in.

FIVE KEY COMPONENTS

To be clear, we're not trying to tell you what types of ministries you need to have or how you should make these decisions in your own setting. We're not saying that all a church should provide is small groups, or that it's wrong to serve the poor or have a baseball team or a junior high fundraiser. Jesus himself made disciples using a variety of methods and activities, yet his goal was always discipleship. He wanted to raise up his men to spiritual maturity, but his disciples weren't always sitting around in a living room with a cup of coffee and a curriculum guide in their hands. To answer Edward's, Rosalie's, and Butch's questions—a men's quartet, a monthly women's gathering, or a coed college baseball team might all be valid ministries within a church, with one caveat. The ministries must all foster environments (or point people to environments) where disciples are made.

For a ministry to be aligned with other ministries around the common mission of making disciples, it must include the following five key components, or it should be a stepping-stone that leads people to another ministry in the church where these components are present.

1. *A clear goal of discipleship.* A ministry should exist to help people follow Jesus, be transformed by him, and join him on his mission. Before you allow someone to start or join a ministry, he should understand this basic goal and define it as

you do. He also needs to be willing to live it out, or you will have real issues before long.

2. *An intentional leader who makes disciples.* A ministry should have an intentional disciple-making leader. The leader should be committed to the disciple-making process and intentional about leading people involved in the ministry to greater spiritual maturity.

3. *A biblically relational environment.* As we've said before, the key factors that cause spiritual growth are the Word of God, the Spirit of God, and the people of God. So each ministry of your church should incorporate each of these key factors. Good teachers will facilitate discussion in which people are free to express themselves. They use the Word but involve everyone in a variety of ways. Good teaching doesn't just inform the head; it also seeks to affect a person's heart and hands. Spiritual maturity and transformation is the goal. Ministries shouldn't just be focused on filling heads with biblical facts. They should show how biblical truth relates to the real needs in people's lives.

4. *A reproducible process.* Those who are involved in the ministry should be growing spiritually in such a way that they are producing more disciples. It might be helpful to walk people through the four-stage process that Jesus modeled for his disciples (SCMD). You may want to teach people the five stages of spiritual growth so they can help those they work with grow to spiritual parenthood.

5. *A supporting organization.* The church as a whole must undergird and communicate the vision that God has given it. This support and communication must happen over and over again. There must be a system that includes job descriptions, and there must be accountability that ensures that what is valued is achieved. Ministry leaders need to constantly be encouraged and coached. The leaders of a church are the ones who protect the church from competing views and ensure that each of their ministries is focused on making disciples. Victories are celebrated in front of the whole church.

When you have all five of these key components in place, that ministry is aligned with the disciple-making process.

Changing an entire church into a disciple-making church is hard work. The more entrenched in tradition a church is, the more difficult it is to align the various ministries together around a common purpose. It's hard to teach old dogs new tricks. And it's also true that some people will have become accustomed to being spiritual children and will not want to see things change. Unfortunately, in some churches the leaders are immature and will not be interested in making these shifts. If this is true in your case, you may need to focus more on planting new churches or doing some of this through less disruptive, unofficial channels. The truth is that no one can stop you from making disciples, but they can stop you from making it the official mission of the church. If this is true in your setting, you will need to humbly rely on the Holy Spirit to give you direction, and to seek wise counsel from others who have made the transition to be disciple-making churches in other places.

BECOMING A MASTER OF ALIGNMENT

As difficult as it is to bring this sort of alignment to a church, I want to encourage you that alignment can happen in established churches; it just takes more work. As with any change, you want to start slowly. Don't make any big changes tomorrow. Get your leadership team to join you in prayer as you slowly work to build alignment and relationship, starting at the top. Build your plans together and seek to understand your context and how these principles apply to your church and skill sets. We do church as a team, which means there is no one person dictating change. Look to the Word to discover these effective visionary principles with your people, and allow them to name these principles whatever they want.

Remember, change starts with the leaders. Always cast vision, first with your actions and then with your words, before making any change. Tell your people why you're going to do something, and reinforce to them what the benefit will be. And then do one piece at a time. Avoid sweeping change in a church. It's okay for alignment to happen in bits and pieces. You might not change your whole church, but at least you can change a large part of it.

For instance, your church might have a men's ministry that's dedicated to community outreach. Once a month, all the men gather and help single moms or the elderly fix their gutters or clean out their yards or rake their leaves. If all the men do is yard work, then that's not an environment for discipleship. But if the five key components are present—if the goal is discipleship, if intentional leaders work with the men in smaller relational environments to help them grow spiritually, if biblical teaching takes place with a strong emphasis on application, if the process is reproducible, and if the process is supported as a whole—then I'd say this is a ministry worth keeping. Or if the community outreach funnels men into other existing biblical relational environments at your church, then it's also worth keeping. Men can come to the outreach event, get connected with other men, and then be encouraged to join a small group.

Or take the average adult Sunday school class. There's no reason why a Sunday school class can't become a place where real discipleship occurs. Don't worry about what you call it—call it Sunday school—but instead of having a teacher stand at the front and impart Bible knowledge, make it a place where all five components are present. Have the teacher introduce the morning, then break up into small groups, with each group led by a maturing facilitator-leader, and encourage authenticity within the interaction around God's Word. Encourage the leaders to go beyond the small group time to do life with those they lead. Encourage them to shepherd the hurting, to develop emerging leaders, to chase the strays. Again, no matter what you call it, it is now a group that leads people to maturity. It may be very wise of you not to radically change the system all at once, yet with small changes here and there, you can take steps to build the components for alignment into your existing structures.

I just helped lead a group of people from Real Life to Israel. At first glance, it might have seemed as if the trip were all about visiting a different country to see the biblical sites. But the trip was really a way of engaging in discipleship. We made sure that the goals of the trip were aligned with the overall purpose of our church.

Several graduating seniors from a local school went, and we got to do devotions at every site with them. They participated by doing some leading and seeing some sites on their own. Each day of the trip, all the team members were on the bus together and were having meals together. There was a devotional guide that got people digging into Scripture. Each day we were praying together, talking about Jesus and his life and ministry. Several parents brought one of their children, and in the evenings while they were in their rooms together, there were some great discussions and times of prayer. Part of our team went on to train pastors in Israel, and some of the kids got to watch their fathers lead these groups. During the trip, my middle son, Jesse, decided that he wanted to become a missionary someday, and when we got home, he led our family through the content we had taught to the pastors on our trip.

Each week at our church, we open our doors to hurting people who come for financial assistance, counseling, and the food room. Thousands each month come for help, and we also have volunteer pastors who come to meet them where they are at. They do the financial counseling and pray with them, and many have come to know Jesus because of this volunteer team. Every week, it seems, we hear over the loudspeaker that we are invited to go downstairs for another baptism. People are helped with their physical needs, but they are also pointed to their real need for Jesus. Every week volunteers are trained and given the opportunity to be used by God to start discipleship relationships with people who are hurting. Our home groups are given the names of people in their area whom they can connect with so they can continue watering the seed that was planted. Many of the volunteers take these new people to their home groups, where they get to take them to the next step (Connect) on their journey.

Just the other day I was walking through the lobby where this ministry is working, and as an experiment, I asked a volunteer why she was doing all this. She was an older woman, and she gave me a big smile. "I'm doing this because we get to help people," she said. "And when we help people, we get to tell them about Jesus, and maybe they'll become disciples."

I asked her how she was being fed spiritually, and she told me that she got together with other people on her ministry team before they opened the doors to the hurting, and they spent time together as a group. She and her husband were also in a small group on Monday nights with some of the other volunteers. I asked her how long she had been doing this, and she said for several years. I then asked her if she ever felt overworked or burned-out working with so many hurting, needy people. She was emphatic in saying that she couldn't imagine her life without her involvement in the ministry. The people she worked with were her closest friends, and she was amazed that God allowed her to serve the hurting with other believers she loved.

She had caught the vision.

KEY POINTS

- Good people want to do a whole bunch of good things, and if a church isn't careful, it's easy to start up a smorgasbord of ministries and go a hundred different directions all at once. There is only so much energy in the church, and we must direct our people to things that make the biggest difference.

- Instead of busying themselves with well-intentioned yet haphazardly focused activities, churches should make an intentional shift to focus on biblical relational discipleship. Making disciples is the main reason why a church exists, so everything in a corporate body needs to funnel people toward the relational small group, where discipleship can best happen.

- When someone asks you if he can start a ministry at your church, or if your church wants to partner with another ministry in town, if those ministries don't align with your overall goal of making biblical disciples in relational environments, then it's okay to say no to the requests.

- For any ministry to take place in a church, it must have five key components, or it must lead people to another ministry in the church where these components are present. The five components are: (1) a clear goal, (2) an intentional leader, (3) a biblically relational environment, (4) a reproducible process, and (5) a supporting organization.

Chapter 10

THE RELATIONAL SMALL GROUP
What actually happens in a small group?

This week, I received an email from one of our regional small groups pastors (community pastors). He wrote to share some of the success stories that are happening at his church plant right now.

- One woman has recently come to church. She's a brand-new believer and wants to be baptized. She's eager to get connected to a home group. There are three home groups really close to where she lives. Any of these three groups would be a good fit for her.

- One of the home groups recently did some major ministry. The apprentice is friends with a couple in which the husband was addicted to meth, so the apprentice moved the wife and two kids into her home to keep them safe. Two weeks later the husband attended their home group, with positive results. Because of what he experienced, he decided to get into a clinic in a nearby town that specializes in addictions. Last Saturday, the home group members rented a trailer and helped move the family's stuff into it because their old lease was up and they needed a new place to live. The group is really helping this family along.

- One home group has begun to provide food for our church ministry that serves the homeless each week. As the result of a sermon series, the group was moved to action and began a benevolence fund to build up money and resources to help people when the needs arise. They are holding garage sales to raise extra money and still giving to the corporate church fund as well.

I share these stories not to boast about our church's reach but simply to show that making disciples in biblical relational contexts can work well to reach the world for Jesus, one person at a time. I might add that these people are not just helping the needy; they meet weekly for spiritual growth, and as they grow and are strengthened, the overflow leads to service and the discipling of others. They are not just being poured *out* through ministry — a trend that happens in some ministries designed solely to meet needs — they are being poured *into* through the weekend services and their small group relationships.

That's the rest of what this fourth shift — from activity to relationship — is all about. Programs in a church don't exist simply so a church can be busy doing good things. That's ineffective. Making disciples is the main reason why a church exists, so everything in a corporate body needs to funnel people toward a relational small group in which discipleship can best happen. While small groups are not the *only* ministry in the church, they are the primary means of making disciples who make disciples. We've spent lots of time talking about the importance of relational small groups, but what specifically needs to happen in a small group for life change and growth to occur?

Ask/Dr. Coleman

What needs to happen — and not happen — in a small group?

There are all kinds of small groups, so what needs to happen may depend on the nature of the group. That needs to be clear when a group forms. Often a group starts one way — fellowship, for instance — yet then it turns from a fellowship time into a prayer meeting. Or it turns from a Bible study into an outreach-oriented group. At least the group itself knows why it exists. Unless that is clear, you can get into problems later on.

When I lead a small group, I like to make it clear as soon as possible what the spiritual reason for the group is. Now, sometimes you don't start there. Sometimes you might just get together for pizza, to get acquainted, to find out where everybody is. But the time will soon come, I trust, when even that beginning will give an opportunity to say, "Would you like to get together sometime to find out what the Bible says on subjects?" If someone says sure, that sounds interesting, you can begin to agree on a purpose.

A group needs to know what it exists for. If not, it will probably wander aimlessly, which leads to frustration. A group in some measure will involve a component of discipleship, even if it's just at the relational level of getting acquainted. There has to be a sense of mutuality, or else you don't have a group. That relationship is the glue that holds it together.

With the group of students I meet with, the relationship centers on a desire to study the Bible, with an eye to growing spiritually and developing a lifestyle of discipleship. To that end, we accept a discipline to pray privately for half an hour each day, commit to read two or more chapters in the Bible, and perhaps memorize a verse or two each week. All the time, we seek to encourage each other to find practical ways to bring discipleship into our daily lives, giving special attention to the family.

With the group of peers and older men I meet with, our purpose is simply to share together, have a Bible study, and pray. And, as we are able, we try to keep in touch with one another, which brings a measure of accountability. That's all our group is. It's very simple. Everybody understands it.

Yes, I've been involved in groups that I've considered a waste of time. Sometimes it's because the group never got to the point where it was a genuine camaraderie of people. I remember once, in seminary, trying to get the whole student body involved in groups. In a prayer meeting, I asked everyone to count off to twelve, then meet with persons who had the same number. Not a good way to create groups. They all got together for a while, but soon they fell apart. Groups need to be Spirit-led to last.

COMPONENTS OF A SMALL GROUP

The relational small group forms the backbone for discipleship. A small group may meet weekly at someone's house or on the weekends at a church building. The key is that the small group's purpose is defined as encouraging discipleship—not primarily fellowship or counseling or even outreach (although these may be vital components of the process).

Let's consider some of the specific components that make a small group an effective tool for disciple making.

Shepherding

A small group is a place where shepherding takes place.

A leader of a small group is a shepherd. He models shepherding for the group, and he seeks to create an environment in which people shepherd one another. In the end, he seeks to teach the group's members to become shepherds themselves in their families and in future groups they may lead.

Ezekiel 34:2–5 describes the shepherding process from the negative perspective of leaders who aren't doing what they need to. The shepherds of Israel are rebuked for their lack of care for the people.

> Son of man, prophesy against the shepherds of Israel; prophesy and say to them: "This is what the Sovereign LORD says: Woe to you shepherds of Israel who only take care of yourselves! Should not shepherds take care of the flock? You eat the curds, clothe yourselves with

the wool and slaughter the choice animals, but you do not take care of the flock. You have not strengthened the weak or healed the sick or bound up the injured. You have not brought back the strays or searched for the lost. You have ruled them harshly and brutally. So they were scattered because there was no shepherd, and when they were scattered they became food for all the wild animals."

The Bible uses sheep to make this point about shepherding. But people, of course, are not livestock. So the challenge to us is to develop practical applications of what shepherds of people should do. Let's examine that passage with an eye to application.

When it comes to "strengthening the weak," a shepherd might have people in his small group who are overwhelmed with life. He could spend time with them and remind them of ways God has provided in the past. He may call to encourage and pray with a person who is struggling; he may ask someone else in the group to use their past history with the same issue to encourage that person. Remember, we create a shepherding culture so we ask people to care for one another in the group. As they use their past for God's glory, they learn to become ministers.

With "healing the sick" and "binding up the injured," Jesus is the good and true shepherd who heals people's illnesses and binds up their wounds (John 10; Matt. 9:36; 11:1–6); however, we can pray for those who are sick or injured, and God, at times, does act to heal. What we can do is care for those who are sick. The small group can do so many things to help when there are struggles. Maybe the group takes turns driving them to the doctor, or brings meals to their house. Healing the sick isn't limited to physical sickness; there may be someone who is dealing with addiction, and we may have to walk them through spiritual healing from the sin that ravages their spiritual and emotional lives. Scripture tells us to carry one another's burdens, and we can do that in so many ways (Gal. 6:2).

With "bringing back the strays," perhaps someone has left the group and appears to be moving away from Christ. Members of the group are encouraged to pray for the one who might be drifting, and the leader will call to check on them. He will encourage those who know the person best to track them down and encourage them to come back to their spiritual family. I often use the analogy with our staff that the church service and small group can be likened to a watering hole. If I have a thousand acre ranch and one watering hole, I can keep track of my cattle in a couple of different ways. I can figure out how to cover every corner of the ranch to make sure all the cattle are okay, or I can just wait by the watering hole to see who shows up. I know the cattle need water or they will die. So as the cattle come in, I can know they are at least okay. I can check on them and look them over. But for the cattle who don't show up, I can know that they are probably in trouble somewhere and that I need to go after them. In the same way, people need spiritual water. When they decide not to come, it tells me something. They have changed their priorities and are drifting. Maybe they are hurt somewhere or lost, so I need to go after them. So many leaders in the church today do not feel the need to chase the strays. They think their job is to build a program, and "if people come, they come." But that is not Jesus' example. Jesus is willing to leave the ninety-nine to find the one, and we should be willing to do the same.

As for the injunction to "not rule them harshly and brutally," all spiritual leadership should be based on grace and truth; the purpose is to love those who stray back into the family. Even when discipline is required, it is for the purpose of restoring, not punishing.

Note the tremendous importance of shepherding being a shared practice. First Peter 5:4 indicates that Christ is the primary shepherd of his people. So the role of a small group leader is to cooperate with Christ in the shepherding process. A leader must encourage all members of the group to become shepherds themselves. In order to create an effective relational environment, leaders intentionally guide their small group members into caring for one another. A leader models what playing together as a team looks like, and helps prepare each person to play his or her part. A leader comes alongside to coach people when they stumble or fall. Together the group members care for each other, and they go after people who stray or lose their way.

Recently I heard of a powerful example of group members shepherding each other in one of our small groups. A couple became pregnant with their first child and the wife gave birth, but then five days later the baby died. It was a devastating and traumatic time for all. Time passed, and as the one-year anniversary of the baby's birth came up, the couple's small group got together and bought a special gift. The group met on the church property along with the couple and planted a tree. The couple and the small group dedicated it in memory of their child. The couple expressed how much that act meant to them.

Ask/Dr. Coleman

Are there some methods that are better than others at getting people into small groups?

When a person comes into the church, it needs to be communicated and understood that this is a relationally oriented church — a pastoral church in which people pastor each other.

Groups can be built around common interests. For some, it might be a youth fellowship or a choir group or even a Boy Scout troop. Yet the groups in a church must all lead to discipleship. It's fine to expect that of people coming into the church. Put it up front, that it's part of their commitment when they join that fellowship.

This church I mentioned in Singapore, it's a church built on the concept of discipleship. Everybody goes through a period of training and comes under the care of a mentor, which ultimately leads them to mentor another person.

Now, churches need to work it out the best way they can do it. Here's where the pastor, in consultation with his elders or board or leadership team, must work out a plan. They go with the plan as long as it seems to be working. If it's not working, they analyze what needs to be changed.

The thing about small groups is that you can change them quite quickly. I think it's good to have periodic evaluations within a group, maybe every three months. Certainly every six months. Ask yourself, Are we fulfilling our purpose? Are we getting out of this what we thought we'd get out of it? If not, then find out what's missing and correct it, or disband the group. Start over again.

Many groups run their course in a few months. Certainly a few years. It's perfectly okay to end a small group. Sometimes it's the best thing you can do. A group is wise when they come to that point and take action.

If you have a termination point in advance, say in six months or a year, then a person is not as hesitant to get involved. For my groups, I ask my students to commit for a semester. They know that's all that is initially expected. This appeals to me because I hesitate to get involved in something that goes on and on. You never know if it's over, and it's embarrassing finally if you say you're going to stop.

Teaching

A small group is a place where real teaching takes place, with Q&A, modeling, and with the best curriculum in the world (the Bible), people can really learn to understand Scripture and use it wisely in their lives.

When people hear about small groups, they often think immediately, *Oh, it's a Bible study.* And that's true in part, but that also needs clarification. Yes, a group must be grounded in biblical teaching. The Word of God, along with the Spirit of God and the people of God, are the three primary components in affecting life change.

But when people think of Bible studies, they often think of a teacher teaching and everyone else passively listening. This is a problem for several reasons. First, many people do not have the gift of teaching, and a person who cannot teach can make a group really boring—and when it's boring, no one comes. Second, it's difficult to recruit leaders, because many will feel that they are unqualified, that they don't have the theological training or biblical knowledge to lead. Remember that we want to develop a method that enables reproduction. If the gift of teaching is required to teach in the small group setting, then reproduction of disciples who can disciple others will be a very slow process. In giving his disciples the Great Commission, Jesus implied that all who follow him, regardless of whether they can teach, can be involved in making disciples.

When I speak of teaching in the small group setting, I mean that there is a leader who shares from God's Word, but it is much more than that. Biblical small groups are more about facilitating a biblical discussion than about directly lecturing. The leader must help group members interact with the Word and with others so that people are participating. It is only when people share their thoughts and ask their questions that I, as a leader, can truly know how they are understanding what God's Word or my small teaching part has meant to them. We have our leaders work from biblically based curriculum so that almost every leader is trained and is able to walk a small group through a discussion. We also encourage a method of discussion generation called "storying," which I discuss in depth in the book *Real-Life Discipleship*.[36]

The key with discussion, after listening to a person share, is always to point people back to God's Word. Jesus is our strength, and his Word is the plan. Whatever life issues a person is working through, point the person to what the Bible says about it. As a leader, you want people to go to Christ, to abide in Christ and in his Word. He gives strength and direction in whatever sphere of life people are dealing with.

Authenticity and Accountability

A small group is a place where authenticity and accountability are encouraged and modeled. We must remember that love is the foundation. Only with this foundation can there be healthy accountability.

When people sin or walk through struggles, the devil tries a couple of different ways to get them separated from God and others. Often, he will try to convince people that what they've done is worse than what anybody else has done. When you believe you are awful, you become ashamed. When this happens, we don't come to God, because we think we are unworthy and that we have blown it too many times to be forgiven. So we are separated from the life in Christ for which we were saved. When shame takes over, we tend to stay away from believers as well. We may even think they are judging us, but this is often because of the shame we feel ourselves. We assume that others feel the same way. The enemy loves to separate us from other believers because he knows that without spiritual friendships, we have no real wisdom or protection (Eccl. 4:9ff). At other times, the enemy will try to tell us that no one has it as rough as we do. In these cases, he is trying to get us to believe that we are justified in our sin and that God understands and even approves. Again, the enemy is seeking to destroy your close relationship with God, and the unrepented of and unconfessed sin is enough to build a wall between us and God. Other times, he will get you to believe that everyone is doing it, so it's not that big of a deal. As people share with one another, they discover that they are not the only ones struggling with an issue, and the shame that keeps them from seeking God or asking people to help is taken away. When they are tempted to give in to temptation and they discover that what they are doing is not something everyone does and that the temptation has been defeated by others, then they can be lifted out of the trees to see the forest.

Sharing breaks the power of secrecy in people's lives. They are freed up from the solitude of going the road alone, and others can encourage them in the journey of faith and in resisting temptation. Always, when people share difficult issues, you want to encourage your group members not to judge but to praise them for bringing things out of the darkness and into the light. Galatians 6:2 encourages us to bear one another's burdens. This is what a small group is about. You want to mourn with those who mourn and rejoice with those who rejoice.

When real-life issues are shared in a small group, sensitivity and tact are needed in big ways. Too often, group members will immediately want to fix other people's problems. But we encourage small group leaders to train their people not to be fixers.

Be listeners first.

Be gentle and empathize, because you yourself know you have your own issues and your own past to deal with.

Be people who pray.

And be people who point others to God's Word.

Note that a leader must encourage transparency for the right reasons. Sometimes people share simply for the sake of being sincere or authentic, or because it is a value of the group and they want to feel included and affirmed. But that doesn't go anywhere if the heart behind it is not being transformed. The reason to be transparent is to take the next step and be the kind of person Jesus wants you to be. That's why a disciple-making group needs a level of honesty and vulnerability that goes beyond what happens at a typical Bible study group. But it also needs to be a place where accountability is expected and given. Love is the foundation, and accountability is one of the parts of loving another person well.

For instance, a while back I was leading a men's small group in which a guy shared about his struggle with pornography. "Thanks for sharing that," I said. "That took courage, and there are others in this group who have dealt with the same thing." I then asked if one of the guys who had dealt with that would share about his journey. As he shared, he made it clear that someone had come alongside him to hold him accountable to change. When he was finished, I looked at the man and asked, "What are you going to do about it? How will you allow us to help you overcome this?"

"What do you mean?" he said.

"Remember, I said several guys in the group here struggle with that same problem. So you heard what they have done. Can we help you do that as well? We've set up filtering and accountability software. It sounds like that might be the next step for you."

"Oh, I'm not sure if I'm ready for that," the guy said. He made it clear through his body language and his voice that he was getting something he didn't want. In other words, he was frustrated by our pressing him to take the next step. He seemed to think that we would be happy with his honesty, but he really had no intention of stopping his habit. Later I called him, and we talked more.

I explained that releasing a secret is the first step, but not the end. People need to make a plan, move forward, and grow.

One more point, and this is also key. Yes, a radical transparency is needed in effective small groups, but yes, transparency needs to happen within boundaries. Boundaries might include gender-appropriate matters. Or sharing things in such a way that confidences aren't broken. Your group can help set the boundaries for what's appropriate.

STORIES OF EFFECTIVENESS

There is no cookie-cutter mold for a small group. They will look different from each other and from church to church. Your church might call the groups by different names—small groups, support groups, care groups, life groups—it doesn't matter. The important part is that a small group is a biblical relational environment in which discipleship takes place. That's the shift that needs to be made.

I asked Gene Jacobs, lead pastor at Real Life Ministries in Silver Valley, Idaho, to talk about some of the challenges and successes he's seen in leading a church based on the relational discipleship model. He and his core group of about twenty-five people planted the church in 2007.

Gene wrote,

> We had advantages right off the bat. We had an old, four-thousand-square-foot building to meet in that had been converted to include a café and thrift store from which to minister to the needs of people and connect them to the body of Christ. The hope was to show them we were not just another church but desired to invest in the community. We also had a huge challenge; we wanted to show people that their idea of what Jesus' church looked like might not be entirely accurate. There might be something more than just showing up every Sunday, putting a couple dollars in a bucket, and listening to a pastor tell them about how he gets to minister to people.
>
> Our church plant started with a meeting over dessert. The café and thrift store had just opened for business. Real Life had expanded their thrift store from Post Falls (forty-five miles away) and was moving toward a new church in this small town in the mountains. We asked the core group to invite as many people as

they knew and to bake some pies. We had about forty people show up. I attempted to answer two questions for them: "Who am I?" and "What am I here for?" I spent some time telling my wife's and my story and how Jesus not only healed a broken marriage but also called us into ministry. My wife and I had both come up through the Real Life Ministries discipleship system and were serving on staff in Post Falls. It was important to establish a pattern for authenticity from moment one.

One of the first questions brought up was, "When do Sunday services start?" You could have heard a pin drop when I explained that we weren't going to start with services right away. Instead we wanted to start small groups and get to know one another beyond just the surface. We were going to learn to do life together the way Jesus did with his disciples.

Each week new people were being invited to join our group. We started identifying and investing in new small group leaders, and more groups began. They were given an opportunity to practice facilitating small group conversation and begin shepherding their small group. The leaders were encouraged to call the group during the week and talk about what Jesus was doing in their lives. Some nights when we got together, very few people would show up, but we would do our best to call the missing and encourage one another.

We have seen God show up in some amazing ways. One of the first people we met in the Valley was Susie. She had lived a hard life and met Jesus in jail. Immediately Jesus started to change her life. As she likes to say it, "Everything started to become clear." Our small group of people welcomed Susie with open arms and did everything they knew to do to show her the love of Jesus no matter what. She was also one of our first baptisms.

With two other of our people, Jim and Sherrie, Jim is one of the quietest guys I have ever met. God has used him and Sherrie to lead a care group that ministers to widows and divorcees in our church in an incredible way. Recently Jim had to spend some time in the hospital, and his group would not allow him to cancel on them for the night; they just got together in his hospital room and met anyway. God has used normal people to show the love of Christ to hurting people and to equip them to love others.

The issue we are always facing and battling is vision drift when it comes to relational discipleship. It seems that some weeks everything comes against the simplicity of following Jesus together. Busy lives, marital issues, sins, people who want the big show. All these things are challenging for the person who's trying to learn how to follow Jesus and really love others. These are the people in our churches.

But as leaders, we have to stay true to what Jesus calls us to in the Bible, no matter what. No matter what people say, no matter who leaves your church, no matter how many times you mess it up. You have to keep pounding the drum of making disciples in relational environments. You have to keep living it out yourself, no matter how tired you get or how hopeless it seems.

That's what I'm talking about. Relational discipleship is Jesus' plan. There is no Plan B. God will bless his plan, and he is responsible for the results.

I am so glad Jesus is in charge of his church. Even with all the challenges godly leaders such as Gene Jacobs face, Gene has told me how blessed he feels that he gets to be a minister in the local church.

The people who are part of Gene's church have become like family. And like most families, they sometimes have disagreements, but they are learning to work through them and love each other no matter what happens. It's the same in our church. Hopefully, it will be the same in yours.

If that all seems a bit messy, it is. The work of disciple making is both great and difficult at the same time. But, as we'll see in the next chapter, that's all part of a new scorecard for success.

KEY POINTS

- Making disciples in biblical relational contexts can work well to reach the world for Jesus, one person at a time.
- The relational small group forms the backbone for discipleship. A small group may meet weekly at someone's house or on the weekends at a church building. The key is that the small group's purpose is defined as encouraging discipleship—not primarily fellowship or counseling or even outreach (although these may be vital components of the process).

- A biblically based, disciple-making small group involves three components. It's (1) a place where shepherding takes place, (2) a place where real teaching takes place with Q&A, modeling, and stories, and (3) a place where authenticity and accountability are encouraged and modeled.

SHIFT

5

From Accumulating
to Deploying

Chapter 11

A NEW SCORECARD FOR SUCCESS

How do we measure success?

Before I became a senior pastor, I worked in youth ministry for several years. As part of my job, I regularly reported to the church board, as well as informally to parents and other church members who phoned me to share what they thought was lacking or working in what I oversaw.

Assessment and evaluation was part of the job. It didn't matter too much what events we organized or what programs we ran; the youth ministry was always evaluated, and I would get asked the same four questions, even though the questions were phrased differently by various people.

- How many kids attended the event?
- How many kids got saved?
- How many kids rededicated their lives?
- How's your budget?

A similar line of questioning has followed me to the senior pastorate. At Real Life, we've tried to do a good job of casting the vision for a new scorecard for success, so people don't ask me these questions so much anymore. The people who do ask them are usually new to our church, or they are colleagues in other areas of the country who inquire about Real Life.

The questions today are,

- How many people attend your church?

201

- How big is your church's budget?
- How big is your building? (or, How many services do you run each weekend?)
- How many people get saved?

Author and pastor Bill Hull, in his book *The Disciple-Making Pastor*, refers to this line of questioning as "the holy trinity of Bodies, Bucks, and Buildings."[37]

Evaluation happens in a church, and it's not wrong. It's actually healthy. But what I'm getting at is that people base their evaluation of a church's effectiveness on the only scorecards they know. It's not wrong to ask about number of services, amount of budget, or size of building, but the problem is that by itself, this scorecard doesn't reflect the most important thing: whether disciples are being made.

Our scorecard for success is too limited, and that needs to shift.

THE CHALLENGES OF EVALUATION

How can you effectively evaluate the success of your church?[38]

It can be tricky to quantify the results of discipleship, because spiritual maturity is revealed in fruit of the Spirit (characteristics such as love, joy, and peace) and in levels of devotion to Christ. Spiritual development shares many characteristics with physical development. In your children's lives, you assess and celebrate different things. You celebrate when they're born, when they take their first steps, when they graduate from kindergarten, when they graduate from high school, when they get married, when they have a child, and so on. You do so, however, with the thought in mind that they have farther to go, they will need to grow more, and they will have to face other challenges. That's why it can be tricky to quantify the results of discipleship — people are always in the process of growing spiritually, so it becomes a now-and-farther-to-go paradox.

When we evaluate, we must make the shift from just attracting and gathering to developing and releasing as well — that's what this fifth and final shift is all about. We call this the shift from accumulating to deploying, because discipleship must result in Christians living out their maturity by showing Christ's love to the world. As healthy Christians are reproducing other healthy Christians, and as healthy churches are reproducing other healthy churches, we will be deploying more and more people into the world to both demonstrate and tell others of the reality of Christ's salvation and kingdom.

This new "release scorecard" is focused on how many people are released as growing and thriving "head, heart, and hands" Christians. I am not saying that they are being released from the body of Christ so they can go start a new one. By deploying (or releasing), I mean they walk out of the discipleship process equipped and motivated to share their faith with the lost wherever they work or live or go to school — any place they interact with other people. They are also able to do life with other believers in relationship. They understand that they are ministers who serve wherever they go in the world. They are becoming people who make disciples at home, love a lost and hurting world, and win people to the Lord and disciple them as they serve as missionaries in the communities where they live.

A release scorecard measures the most important things, and when these become what you strive for and celebrate, your church will produce empowered Christians who are able to change the world. This process transforms individuals, homes, places of work, and communities because rather than gathering and acquiring an audience, you have released an army on your community. The answer to the question of how to effectively evaluate the success of your church goes to the heart of everything we've been talking about in this book. It is more important to evaluate how many people go out than to evaluate how many show up.

To clarify, I'm not against having a building that people come to. I am just against a building people come to where there is no discipleship process. I am not against counting the numbers of new converts or of people's rededications, examining budgets or the size of buildings, or asking about how many services a church runs each weekend. But I take all that information in context. I'm more about what is happening in and through all those things. I am concerned about training up people and releasing them.

So often, the most frustrated leaders are the ones who would be counted as winners on the faulty scorecard we have been talking about. I see this all the time in the churches that come to our train-ing seminars at Real Life. We hear church leaders say, "It's not work-ing." They're frustrated, stressed, tired, and nearing burnout because the people they serve are acting like children. They have gathered a huge crowd of spiritual infants and children, and with more children come more problems. So many people in churches are saying, "Feed me," and "I don't like that food," and "The music isn't good," and … and … and … The leaders of these churches often know they have not been defining success God's way. They've falsely defined discipleship as the transfer of information, and when they evaluate success the way they've always done, frustration eventually results. It's sad to me that the pastors that are saying this are the pastors whom all the other leaders put on a pedestal. In other words, the smaller churches want to be like the bigger churches, and the bigger church leaders are ready to pull their hair out.

Sometimes board members come to the training seminars too. In some cases, the only evaluation tools they are familiar with are busi-ness models of evaluation. They run a paint store or are a midlevel manager at an insurance company, so they're familiar with models of acquisition and achievement, and they apply these models to the church. Or sometimes the problem is multiplied because they've read a book or article or see big crowds listening to a famous pastor, so they falsely conclude that since the guys at the megachurch are doing this, (whatever the newest "this" is), then they need to do it too. Or they evaluate based on personal comfort. If they didn't like the music last week, or the sermon the pastor preached, then they'll put pres-sure on their senior pastor to change things so they bring in the big crowds. After all, they conclude, success for a church means getting more people to attend, having a bigger budget, and building a larger building. Again, I am not against better music and better preaching, and it is true that if you have these things, you will have more people. But more people does not necessarily mean better people and more eternal significance.

We get other churches in which the leaders know their church is broken, even by traditional standards. People aren't coming to know the Lord. Numbers are dwindling. The budget is strained and hurting. They haven't had any baptisms for a long while. So their scorecard says, "FAIL," because by every standard measurement, they are ready to shut their doors. They wonder what to do. How can they prop things up, even turn things around? They're keenly aware of the old adage that goes, "People vote with their feet and their checkbook." And often that has become mixed in with their church's scorecard for success. It's true — a church typically has a building, and they've got to pay bills. So if people walk out or stop giving, that puts pressure on the pastor to give the people what they want instead of what they need.

Sometimes church planters come to us with the sincere motivation to create a new and effective church from the ground up. The planter doesn't want the new church to be all about the spiritual experience or event. He wants a new direction and wants to use a new scorecard but doesn't know how to lead toward it or how to get people to think in those terms. Maybe his church is up and running already (say he's got eighty people coming), but he's fighting the old scorecard already. Most of the people have come from other churches, so their scorecard has already been set. They usually left the church they came from because of a previous scorecard developed somewhere else or because one wasn't discipled properly into them, they made up their own, and now they threaten the new work with expectations that are tough to live up to. Whether they came up with their scorecard by themselves or through the TV church they watch, or whatever, it usually has something to do with how they and the masses like coming to the worship service, how many attend a class, and how big the offering is.

One final group we get at our trainings is the big churches who want to figure out our "secret" and apply it to their congregation. They come to our training seminars fully believing that they're pretty successful because they've gathered a large crowd. They tend to just want to get better at small groups so that people have relationship in their larger church. But they hear about discipleship, about a new scorecard for success, and they discover that no one is impressed with their large numbers. They feel convicted and say, "Whoa, okay. People are coming to our church because we've got a good show, but there's little depth. Now what do we do?" They rightly change directions and want to know how to focus less on the events and more on the spiritual maturity of the people they care for.

So what's the solution?

THE PHILOSOPHY BEHIND SCORECARDS

A new scorecard begins to take shape when people in a church begin to think of themselves as spiritual beings who start out as infants when they are born again and are to become spiritual parents in the end. When they understand that this is God's plan for all of us, it changes their perspective. When they understand that every believer is to be a minister who serves Jesus and others with all they have, and then eventually to make disciples themselves, it changes the dynamic of the church. When pastors come face-to-face with this reality, it changes how they see all they do.

The point is that we must champion and reclaim the ministry of all believers.[39] If a church hires a pastor to be a paid performer (they would say "paid teacher") that people want to come and listen to, then the success or failure of a church is all up to him. But if a church hires a pastor to be a coach, then the success or failure of a church is up to the people as well.

Life-changing decisions are supported by accountability and discipline and inspiration that comes through continual relational togetherness. I learned this when I struggled to deal with my alcohol and drug problems. Many times, I was moved emotionally to a decision to stop, but it wasn't until I got together with others and allowed them to help me and encourage me, and even tell me that I was wrong, that real change started to happen. Absolutely, it was Jesus who moved into my heart. He gave the will and strength to change. But God continued to work through others in my life, and that enabled me to come out the other side.

Yes, it takes a while for pastors and Christians to start thinking of themselves as equippers and ministers who make disciples, and this is a vision that needs to be presented to congregations and recast more than once. When people don't have this vision, it becomes evident in the evaluation questions that come back to leaders.

For instance, maybe someone comes to you in the lobby and says, "We haven't seen a baptism in a year at this church. What's the matter, Pastor?" What would you say?

A question like that is an indication that people have been trained to think a certain way and evaluate churches with a certain scorecard for success. The person asks this question because he or she thinks it's the pastor's responsibility to ensure that a steady stream of baptisms occurs, when really the question needs to be put back to the person who asked it. "Well, do you know anyone who's lost? Have you shared the gospel with that person and led him to the Lord?" The person who asked the question is just as much a disciple who makes disciples as the pastor is.

Bringing in a new scorecard for success may be a challenge at first and may cause problems. People have been raised to want something, and they're not going to like being challenged or having things changed.

As with any change, the solution is to cast the vision to your elders first. Build the team. Establish the relationship in which your leaders buy into the vision of what success is and how to make sure you reach it by God's power. The job of a pastor is to lead so that everybody's on the same page, and that sometimes means some effective pruning. It takes time. Before you make any big transitions, you have to get all your leaders to catch the vision.

Ask Dr. Coleman

What does it mean for a church to be successful?

The church is the body of Christ, and you find success in the way that Christ would minister in the context of a group as his body.

In a church, that sense of belonging is much like the sense of being in a family. There is trust in that relationship. A church is fortunate when its board of elders has the solidarity of a family. So is a pastor who has a group close to him with whom he can discuss the problems and triumphs of a church openly. People he can bounce ideas off. People who can correct him.

I define success in the way a church has accepted God's mission as its sense of purpose. Every church has, or should have, a mission statement. The pastor can prepare the people by teaching and preaching God's purpose for the church. This statement gives people something by which to measure their growth and success. It will include what they believe is the will of God for that part of the body of Christ.

You evaluate against your mission, against your purpose.

THE SCMD SOLUTION

Remember when we were examining the principles of Jesus' strategy for making disciples, using a blueprint based on four words: *Share, Connect, Minister, Disciple*?

These same four words become the basis for our new scorecard for success. The questions to ask when evaluating a church are:

- Are we as a church corporately sharing Jesus with people outside our walls? Are we discovering ways to take Jesus to people in the world together? Second, are our people loving a lost and hurting world and sharing their faith wherever they go as individuals? How do I know they are?
- Are we as a corporate body inviting people to connect with Jesus in relational environments? Are our people in small groups? Are our people inviting people to connect with them in their small groups as they live in the world? How do I know this is happening?

- Within those environments, are we biblically training our people to be ministers? Are they becoming ministers in the corporate body and in their small groups? Are they learning that God has gifted them to serve, and are they discovering their abilities? How do I know this is happening?
- As our people are growing in spiritual maturity, are we equipping them to make more disciples? Are new leaders who understand how to lead a disciple-making ministry emerging from our church's ministries? Are our small groups developing new leaders who can make disciples in relational environments? How do I know it is happening?
- Are new, higher-level leaders emerging who can come on staff as full-time, paid leaders? Are new church planters being developed so that the work of Christ becomes more of a movement in the region?

Let's make this practical. Say a staff member at Real Life ran a program, then came back and said, "We had five hundred people make first-time decisions for Christ."

I'd say, "That's amazing. Let's celebrate it. We've just shared Jesus and had a strong response. Now, how many of those new converts are getting connected?"

Perhaps the staff member would answer that 388 people have been connected to small groups so that they can grow in spiritual maturity. I would again say, "Amazing! Let's celebrate that. But it sounds like we have 112 people to track down, and how will we do that?"

Once those people get connected, we'd begin to ask (usually this is a question that gets asked over time) how many of those people are moving into ministry roles. Here I'd say, "Wow, let's celebrate that as a staff and as a church."

Then, over years, we would ask how many people are moving into roles in which they disciple others. We would ask how many new small group leaders have emerged. (This is my favorite celebration, although I like them all.) We would ask how many people God has shown us who have a call to full-time, paid ministry. When this starts to happen, you have a movement on your hands.

At the end of the day, the most important scorecard for success is how many mature disciples your church has developed. You measure success against SCMD criteria. We're not saying that conversion is not part of success. It is part of success. But it's just the first step in the maturing process, not the only step. Back to the analogy of your child's birth. When they are born, you definitely celebrate. But you know that you have not arrived at the end of the journey; you have only passed the first milestone. There are many more important ones yet to come, and you celebrate them as well.

ENLARGE THE FOCUS / NARROW THE FOCUS

When it comes to evaluating a church's success, the overall scorecard relates to the SCMD criteria. Within that criteria, leaders at different levels will ask different things. There has been debate over the years about top-down or side-to-side flowchart-style models of the relationship of a pastor to a congregation, and the point is not to discuss the different models now, but let's just assume a top-down model for a minute.

As a senior pastor, I think in terms of the big picture. I don't want to micromanage; I want to macromanage, so I ask my team the largest questions I can. Questions like,

- How many conversions lately?
- How many people showed up this weekend at church?
- How many people are getting connected to small groups?
- How's the budget doing?
- How are our church plants doing?
- How many coaches do we have at the plants?
- How's the youth pastor doing at developing leaders who can make disciples?
- Is the church actually meeting needs in the community? Or is our church the big-show church that everybody comes to? Is our church actually changing people's lives?
- Are the processes we set up aligning our people?
- How many came to the membership class, and how many got connected from that?

- When it comes to the four spheres, are our people really getting it, or do we have a breakdown in the system?

Absolutely, these questions are only some of the ones that need to be asked. If eight thousand people showed up for weekend services, that number might be celebrated, but I know that just because eight thousand people show up, it doesn't mean we have eight thousand people who can make disciples—and that's what our team is ultimately shooting for.

So who thinks about the individual in church? As a senior pastor, I aim to get an overall view. (I am still in a small group, so I care about the smaller picture too.) I want our small group leaders to have the ground-level view. As we move "downward," we get more specific and personal.

For instance, when I meet with our elders and executive team, we ask big questions, like I mentioned above. But when our executive leaders meet with the community pastors (regional small groups), the questions they ask are narrower and sharper. Our community pastors all have volunteer coaches who care for small group leaders who care for their small groups. So when our community pastors meet, they are asked questions like,

- How are our coaches doing in the four spheres (most important, the first one)?
- How many new coaches are emerging from the small group leader ranks?
- Which of our coaches have higher-leadership ability?
- How many mature group leaders do we have in the community?
- How many small groups are sharing their faith with their neighborhoods?

We move down one more step. When our community pastors and coaches meet, the questions are even more individually based and personal. I want the questions coaches ask to be narrower and sharper still. For instance,

- How are the three small group leaders in this community doing?
- Are any of them struggling?

- How well are the small group leaders caring for their groups?
- Which ones are really doing great, and how do we celebrate that?
- Are our people really growing in the four spheres, and is there one we really need to focus on for someone we're working with?
- Is there a group leader who isn't progressing or is falling back whom we can pray for or need to really help?

Move down yet one more step. I want the small group leaders to ask,

- How are the ten people in my small group doing?
- Which sphere do we really need to deal with in my group?
- Are the people in my group growing spiritually?
- Has anybody been missing for a while? How can we get this person reconnected?
- Who needs to be challenged to minister more?
- Who might be ready to lead a small group soon?

And at the end of the evaluation, I want each Christian to ask,

- Am I growing spiritually? How's my relationship to Christ?
- How do I need to grow up in the family of God?
- How's my family doing? Am I leading them (or supporting them) the way I need to?
- Am I serving where I need to as I minster in the world where I work and live?
- Am I making disciples?

PUTTING IT ALL TOGETHER

How will your church evaluate success?

The point of this shift is that it's not all about gathering a large number of people at your church. That might be fine, but it's only one step in the process. Success means we are training people up in spiritual maturity so they can make more disciples.

Each week at Real Life, we issue a scorecard to ourselves as a church. We talk about it as staff members, and we post it on our website. It's called "The Celebration Report Card," and we don't put it out there to pat ourselves on the back. Rather, it's a strategic part of the evaluation and vision-casting process. It's one of the tools that helps keep our vision always before us, reminding us of what we're continually striving to do.

A recent report card, for instance, talked about our youth ministry. One campus held a film festival night that was attended by 120 college-age people. That was strong attendance, and we celebrated that. But we didn't stop there. We also reported that unconnected kids were invited to make a short movie together with established small groups. Five new leaders were raised up to help with the small groups program.

In another week, more than fifteen hundred people attended a Department of Labor job fair hosted by our church. On that day, twenty new people sought help from our benevolence department and met with one of several "pastors of the day" we have on hand for such events. Some sixty-seven families were assisted with food through our food room and invited to connect with our church. That week, there were eleven decisions to follow Christ, and eight baptisms.

During Easter Week this past year, we ran a community Easter egg hunt. Some 497 families who were previously unconnected to our church attended the hunt along with about five thousand others. From those families, thirty got connected, with eighty-seven kids from those families registering for our children's ministry.

Those are the kinds of evaluations we need in our church.

They ask, What's truly happening? And they help us know what we're doing right, and where we can do better.

Which brings us to perhaps the most practical question of all: how can you begin to implement discipleship in your church? We'll work through that question in the next chapter.

KEY POINTS

- Evaluation happens in a church, and it's not wrong. It's actually healthy. But people base their evaluation of a church's effectiveness on the only scorecards they know. It's not wrong to ask about number of services, amount of budget, or size of building, but the problem is that by itself, this scorecard doesn't reflect the disciple-making process.

- When we evaluate, we must make the shift from attracting and gathering to developing and releasing—that's what this fifth and final shift is all about. Discipleship must result in Christians living out their maturity by showing Christ's love to the world.

- Deploying (or releasing) means that people in your church are equipped and motivated to demonstrate God's love and share their faith with the lost wherever they work or live or go to school—any place they interact with other people. They are also able to do life with other believers in relationship connection. They understand that they are ministers who serve wherever they go in the world. They are becoming people who make disciples at home, love a lost and hurting world, and win people to the Lord as they serve as missionaries in the communities where they live. That's the new scorecard for success.

Chapter 12

MAKING THE "DISCIPLESHIFT" IN YOUR CHURCH

How do you implement discipleship in your church?

In just a few moments, you're going to be finished reading this book. You'll turn the last page and then ask yourself a huge question: now what? In other words, where do you go from here? The biblical purpose of the church is to make biblical disciples in relationship who can make biblical disciples — so how do you do that? What specific steps do you take to begin to implement discipleship in your church?

These are hard questions to answer because I don't know anything about your specific context. In fact, it's more strategic if I don't answer them for you, even if I could. It will be best for your church if you and your leadership team take the principles in this book and wrestle with them as they relate to your unique practices, traditions, and corporate structures, as well as the context you live in. Your town can have a slightly different way of thinking or living than that of a town just a few miles away. Each of us has a different gifting and a way of thinking that makes us unique, and we have a different group of people we do ministry with that makes our situation different from any other. One of the reasons we encourage churches to join the Relational Discipleship Network is because churches need other churches — in relationship together, learning to walk this journey together.[40]

At the same time, my aim has never been to create more churches based on me or Real Life Ministries or our team. I want churches to be created around Jesus Christ and what he says in his Word. I believe that the principles we have looked at are absolutely biblical, so they will work in any context or at any time in history. My belief in that comes from my faith in who Christ is. He is the master designer of people, and he knows how he made them and what they need. If we simply look to him and his Word for answers and then apply those truths wisely in our own context shaped by the teams we do ministry with, then we can start to see the church in our area win again.

In many ways, the fifth and final shift, from accumulating to deploying, encompasses all of the first four shifts. It gets to the heart of the church's main purpose. People don't come to church; people *are* the church. Our big goal isn't to accumulate a crowd and impart information to them. It's not to create an emotional experience that will keep them charged up for a few hours or days and make them want to come back so they can feel it again. The shift is that we need to raise up biblical disciples and deploy them into the world so they can raise up other disciples. These disciples are to grow into accurate copies of Jesus who rightly deliver his message in his ways. I truly believe that if people could see Jesus for who he really is, they would love him. The unfortunate thing is that most people who have rejected him have done so because they've been shown a false Jesus. That's the big question to explore: how do you implement discipleship in your church so your people can experience real faith and reveal the real Christ to the world in a way that glorifies him?

WHERE TO GO FROM HERE

Let's look at five steps you can take to help your church shift toward becoming a church that makes disciples.

Step 1: Develop Biblical Vision

As a team, develop the biblical vision for your church.

Begin the process by bringing together the leaders God has sent you, to look to his Word in order to develop his big picture for the church in your area. Remember that he wants mature disciples who make mature disciples. Come together at a church leadership level and begin to ask big questions together. Achieve consensus regarding vision, as vision comes from God's Word.

When you have discovered his view in Scripture together, start living it out as a leadership team. You cannot give your people something you do not possess. If your team is truly together, you may lose members of the congregation as you lead change, but the church will be intact. Do not try to shift your church as an individual. It's highly important that you shift as a team. You will need each other for encouragement, because it will not be easy to change an existing church. For that matter, it's not easy to start a new church. The unity that you develop at a leadership level will be necessary over the long haul as you work through all of the steps involved. That is the drumbeat you've got to hold to throughout the process of shifting: unity centered on biblical truth.

Remember, you are basing your view of purpose on Jesus and the Scriptures, and that does not change. The specific way you implement things may vary based on context and gifting, but the goal does not change. When people visit Real Life, they often ask me, "Jim, what's your vision for Real Life?" And my answer is that it's not my vision. It doesn't matter what my vision is. It's got to be God's vision for this church, and that is to make disciples who make disciples.

The Bible promises that the gates of hell cannot prevail against Christ's church (Matt. 16:18). It does not promise that the gates of hell will not prevail against my church or your church; the promise is only for *His* church. To repeat: you achieve consensus on vision, as vision comes from the Word.

Pastor and author Sam Rainer developed a list of questions that Bobby Harrington and others have utilized that are helpful to this stage, especially with established churches making these shifts.[41] Bobby adapted Rainer's questions a bit for use at Harpeth Community Church, and, as you study Scripture and lead your team, you might find it helpful to use his version of them, which appears in the following list.

- How does the Bible define discipleship?
- What does the Bible say a disciple looks like?

- What is the discipleship process as we see it happening in Scripture?
- What are the specific phases of discipleship, as seen in the scriptural models?
- How will everyone in our church come to know this process?
- What characteristics (values) must be present for real-life discipleship to occur in our church? (Values include love, acceptance, and accountability.)
- How will our church (at every level) emphasize the discipleship process?
- How will our church practice keep the focus on discipleship by making church "simple" and "clear"?
- How will our church raise up, reproduce, and release disciple-making leaders?
- How will our church serve as an attractional light on a hill?
- How will our church send people out to serve incarnationally in the community?

It is vital that your team develop clarity of vision, because you will need to articulate that vision again and again. A vision statement is not just something you throw on your wall and leave there. Your vision statement is something you pursue fervently over the long haul. Your team will need to develop it together because they need to own it themselves and be able to articulate it with all of those they lead as well. Every leader must have the same vision, as well as methods to accomplish it, and they must speak of it with a common language over and over again.

Keep in mind that a church's vision doesn't change every couple of months with each new conference you go to either. This is important, because there are always new ideas coming down the road, and it's easy to be sidetracked. It's far easier to become too many things to too many people.

True enough, the way a vision is implemented can and will change. It's also true that sometimes a vision drifts, and you will need to deal with the effects of that and correct your course. So one of the questions to consistently ask is, Have we really accomplished our vision? If not, what's gotten in the way of that?

Sometimes structures need to be reorganized and a church's focus needs to be narrowed.

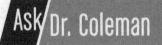

What encouragement would you give to a church that wanted to make the shift to discipleship?

The pastor is key. He is the leader. He is the shepherd. He needs to be very prayerful in terms of how the church moves into its vision.

If you make a transition abruptly, then the probability of some people being offended is high. They weren't consulted. They weren't prepared for it. They might not agree with it to start with. That stance is unprofitable as a rule.

So the pastor, working with his leadership, must develop consensus around a vision. The vision, of course, needs to be in line with God's vision. Together the pastor and leaders determine how they will begin. This doesn't mean that a pastor can't have a strong sense of direction. Far from it. Unless he knows where to go, how can he lead his people?

That's where you begin. Get consensus among the leaders before you start spreading it out from there. If you go outside the consensus of the leadership, you'll cause trouble and create division. The leadership of the church should reflect the aspiration and commitment of the church, and they should understand the cultural setting of the community.

One practical way of progressing is to announce a trial group, just to see how it works. Sometimes it's good to have two or three trial runs before large numbers of people get involved. Then, once you decide what really works, you can begin to multiply the process.

Develop a plan that works. Then enlarge it. When you get enough small groups that are working, you make it a congregational structural practice. By that time, everyone is probably in a small group anyway.

If it's an old situation, it will probably take a long time.

If it's a brand-new church plant, no problem. It's easier to start with something new than to take a fossilized situation and try to change it. It can happen, and I've seen it happen, but it's much slower. Even then it doesn't run as smoothly in the beginning as it does with a plant, where people come in right from the beginning and have an idea of where you're going.

Step 2: Create a Common Language

As a team, create a common language and definition of terms.

People sometimes combine this second step with the first step, but I like to set it apart to shed light on its importance. If you are to succeed as a team, you must create a common language—using the same words and the same definitions. In some ways, this is done in conjunction with forming your vision statement. But in other ways, it comes afterward. Once you come to an agreement together, you are ready to take it to the next level of leadership in your church so that you can get on the same page with them as well.

Practically speaking, when we developed our vision at Real Life, we went through the Bible and said something like, "Well, we can see that the Bible teaches this and this and this, and these things appear to be normative practices for today too. We believe that's God's vision for our church. Now, what would we call these things today in our church?"

Again, the necessity of creating your own common language is highly important. Vision statements do not all need to look the same from church to church, nor should they. They'll look different from my church to your church, and they'll look different from your church to the churches that people in your congregation came from. If you don't carefully articulate your own terminology, people will make up their own based on their past filters and experiences. Yes, it's perfectly fine for churches to not use the same words to describe the same biblical concepts. Our church might use the word *release*. Your church might use the word *deploy*. The principles will still be biblical. But different churches will establish different language. Just make sure everyone in your church agrees on what your language means.

The stakes with common language are high, because when differences in terminology arise within a church, there is great potential for confusion, blame, and even accusations. A few weeks ago I spent an hour and a half in a tense meeting because the people involved were using the same words but defining those words differently. If you don't all define your terms the same way, then one person thinks he's doing what he needs to be doing, but another person disagrees. It can get heated and personal then. People will say, "You're lying," or "You said you'd do something, but now you're not doing it." And the other person may say, "I did exactly what I said I would," and he isn't lying; he was using the same words with different definitions.

Our churches are filled with good-hearted people who want to do the right thing, but if terms aren't defined, church can get rocky, even with the best-hearted people. Remember that we don't simply have a natural world that tears us apart. We have a scheming, spiritual enemy who wants to confuse language and bring doubt and division. The enemy is just waiting to devour (1 Peter 5:8). So it's vital that your church develop common goals, terms, and language and then progress from there. We must constantly clarify, communicate, and have conflict resolution if we are to succeed.

Once, we took our executive team away on a retreat, and as part of the learning experience, our facilitator proposed that we all play a game. First, the facilitator announced that the name of the game was saboteur, and that if we thought we knew who the saboteurs were as the game went on, then we could vote people off the team. In another room, a set of cards was put in a specific order on a table.

Then we had the same cards in a different order on a table in the room where we were. One by one, people were sent into the other room to look at the ordered cards, then came back to reorder the cards in our room in the same order as they saw in the other room. As the game progressed, the cards got messed up. Or at least, various people thought the cards got messed up. We eventually voted four people off our team out of the game. Then the facilitator sat us all down and explained the game's twist. Our team didn't have *any* saboteurs. The game itself was called saboteur, and that was it.

We learned a ton about assumptions during that game. It was so easy to blame other people, to accuse them of messing things up on purpose. Yet we were all trying to help; we just saw things differently. People assumed that just because we saw things differently, other people were *intentionally* trying to mess things up, which wasn't the case at all.

How often does something similar happen in a church? We accuse people of having bad motives, of trying to mess things up. But the mess-ups happen only because we see things differently and again don't define the words we use in the same way. In reality, we often don't assume the best about people. We assume the worst. This is why churches divide and relationships break. Conflict is inevitable in relationships, and we must be committed to working things out constantly; that is a part of spiritual maturity.

Step 3: Develop the Disciple-Making Process

As a team, develop the process for creating disciples, then put this process into the hands of the frontline soldiers.

At this stage, you must do two things. First, you must make sure that the language and process you have developed is easy for your people to understand and to use. Remember, you are equipping your soldiers with weapons they must be familiar with and skilled with. The SCMD process and the discipleship definitions were created with our spiritual soldiers in mind. Second, you must create a process or system for getting your people trained in your language and skills. If you use the soldier analogy, then after you have developed weapons that your men and women can use, you must have a way to train your people how to use them. In the military, this is boot camp, followed by training schools. It has to be done the same way in a church or team.

In order to get everybody on the same page, we use the analogy of a playbook for a football team. If you're a high school football player and you play for one school, then transfer to another school, you still play the game of football, but you're going to encounter a different playbook—the manual that explains the specific and unique way that a particular school plays football.

So how do you successfully play football for that new school? You need to learn their playbook. You need to learn how they do things at that school. What will happen if you don't learn the playbook? If you're in the huddle, when the quarterback calls plays, you won't know what he's saying or what your part on the team is. You need to know the specific system that they run, and you need to know your part in the game.

Our playbook contains several parts. After we've defined terms, we go over methodology. We talk about how disciples are made, and specifically how they are made at Real Life. As people get involved on the team, we then can identify those who have leadership ability and a shepherd's heart. We have a separate playbook just for them, which focuses solely on leaders and explains their functions and roles.

At Real Life, we use the playbook over and over again. If you want to be a leader at Real Life, each year you return to class, study the playbook again, and re-sign our leadership covenant. We have found that it's vital to reinforce the ideas again and again and continually develop consensus. It's like playing football for a school for one year, then coming back the next year. They may have added a few plays in the playbook, or you may have forgotten. So you've got to learn the playbook every year.

Developing this consensus year after year is a particularly important step for church planters, who regularly work with new Christians and with Christians who've transferred from other churches. People either don't know what to do, because they're brand-new, or come to your church with different terminology and different ways of doing things. If you don't get everybody on the same page—and keep getting everybody on the same page—then big problems will arise. People will expect things from you as pastor because they've defined your job in certain ways. Or they will want things they experienced at their other church. If you don't constantly remind them of your playbook, you are in for a real headache.

For instance, a colleague was the worship pastor at a church plant. The preferred methodology of that church plant was to create a blended service with an eye to contemporary worship in order to connect with the people in that region. The worship pastor thought he had communicated this to the church; it was the worship style his boss expected him to implement.

Yet within a month of being there, a woman came to the worship pastor. She'd just visited a new church downtown where they had a twenty-four-hour prayer-and-praise ministry. It wasn't a bad movement, but it was very different from what they were doing at the church plant. The prayer ministry didn't use organized music or musicians, and it was a much more free-flowing expression of worship that happened around the clock. The woman was very excited about the prayer-and-praise ministry, and she had a persistent personality. She insisted that the worship pastor visit the other church to observe the different style. She was convinced that as soon as he saw it, he would want to transition the worship style at the church plant to this other style.

There ended up being a lot of frustration and misunderstanding between the worship pastor and this woman (and also her husband, who took his wife's side). They all had the same goal—to worship God. But their methodology to do that was different, and they couldn't get on the same page. The woman and her husband eventually left the church plant, angry with the worship pastor and convinced he was doing the wrong thing.

If you're a church leader and your church has a playbook, then right up front it helps answer a well-meaning person like this who wants the church to go another direction. It helps articulate to that person the specifics of what you do as a church and why you do it. It helps the church leader say something like, "Hey, that's great that you've experienced something else. But we're going this direction, and here's why."

Step 4: Live Out Your Vision

Consistently live out your vision, and consistently recast your vision.

Once you've got the vision worked out, the terms defined, and the processes established, then it becomes all about implementation. How are you going to ensure that all leaders at all levels live out the vision?

With implementation, the key is to ensure that no matter what the program is at your church, people at every spiritual level accept the practical ramifications of the vision.

If you've got a membership class, it's got to align, and everyone must go through it if they are to serve in the church.

If you've got a home group, it's got to align.

If you've got a youth ministry, it's got to align.

Make sure you're doing what you say to the best of your ability at each level. One of my jobs as senior pastor is to make sure the staff members are aligned with the vision. Sometimes staff members aren't. A while back, the wife of one of my church plant staff members grew angry with her husband's boss (one of the executive-level pastors at Real Life) and wasn't willing to resolve the issue. What made it worse was that they hadn't even let him know that there was a problem, and I heard about it.

I knew I couldn't let that continue. The staff member was one of my best leaders, but we couldn't tolerate divisiveness to the degree it was happening. So I brought the staff member into my office, and we worked it through. As the spiritual leader in his home, he needed to ensure that no root of bitterness grew in his family. He couldn't keep doing his job at the church and yet have unresolved tension. God doesn't bless a church like that. Jesus told his disciples that they shouldn't even bring their sacrifice to the temple if there was unresolved conflict; he said to first go and make it right and then bring the offering. If he didn't want a sacrifice, do we really believe he wants us leading in a church when we haven't done all we can to be in unity with another believer? It was this man's responsibility to resolve the issue, and I gave him a week to do so. The man asked for forgiveness, and fortunately, we worked to resolve the issue.

That's part of living out our vision. Not only do we need to communicate the vision to all levels, but also we use the vision to interact with people on a day-to-day basis. Before we *do*, we must be. As we press into relationship with Jesus, he leads us to be right in the other spheres of our lives.

And vision needs to be continually recast. Continually communicate the vision to your team and your church. Continually live out God's vision for the church and explain to people why you do the things you do.

Step 5: Assess, Correct, and Encourage

Constantly assess, correct course, and encourage.

In this final step, you develop and implement your new scorecard for success. As always, you do this as a team. Your new scorecard should directly correspond to your vision statement. You constantly ask yourself and your team questions such as, Are we doing the vision? How are we doing with living out the vision? Where are we weak? What are we doing that we shouldn't be doing? So often, we are so busy as pastors doing everything that we have no time or ability to assess. This is a real problem. When we are out of balance, we model it as a positive attribute to others, and we create a culture that is unable to self-correct.

Really, there are three parts to this last step.

1. *Assessment.* We honestly evaluate how we're doing as a church against the criteria of our vision.
2. *Course correction.* We're honest with our assessment. If we're not living up to our goals, we admit that, then take steps to get back on track. We say things such as, "Our goals were these, and we weren't doing them. Now let's return to the path we need to be on." We are honest with our people when we have gotten off course, and by being honest, we are vision casting the right course.
3. *Encouragement.* What we celebrate as a church, people aspire to. So we purposely celebrate ministry items that correspond

to our vision. We celebrate whenever God has done something in our church through our people.

Note that with assessment, it's always tempting to want to change your church's vision statement. But I strongly caution you against doing this. Trust the process you've gone through in studying God's Word, defining your terminology, and developing your methodology.

God's vision for your church doesn't change every time you go to a new conference or read a new book. You might need to cut a program, add a new ministry, or align your ministries together, but your overall goal doesn't change.

Stay the course with your vision. And constantly reinforce your vision again and again. I asked my friend Aaron Couch, lead coach of Real Life on the Palouse, a church plant in Pullman, Washington, about the need to reinforce vision.

Aaron wrote,

> Leaders often think that if they cast vision once, it will be immediately understood. But you can never cast vision enough. You've constantly got to reinforce your vision for your people.
>
> For example, after coming to our church for a year and a half, a man came to me one day with a shocking revelation. He said, "You know, I am really starting to realize that getting people into spiritual relationships is critical for their spiritual development."
>
> For a year and a half he had heard nothing other than that. This was a very sharp man, highly intelligent and very successful at business, and he had grown up in the church.
>
> At the age of fifty-five, he suddenly realized that getting people into relationships is critical. It took him a year and a half of hearing that message over and over again to have it sink in.
>
> This example is not uncommon. In fact, I would submit that it will continue to be the norm, particularly for people who have previous church experience.

Ask Dr. Coleman

What's the one thing you'd want people to know about the discipleship process?

While conditions in the world seem to worsen, it's when the night closes in that we can more easily see the stars. If we are moving toward the close of history on this earth, likely things are going to get more difficult than they are now. In such times, the church comes to her finest hour. The greatest days of evangelism are before us.

Our mission is not to a certain geographic locality. The command of Christ is to preach the gospel to everyone, to make disciples of all nations, to be his witnesses in Judea, Samaria, and the ends of the earth. There's no differentiation in the Bible between home missions and foreign missions. That objective is always in view.

And the church is reaching that goal today better than it's ever done, that is, if you go outside of North America and Western Europe. We can all rejoice in the growth. But the great need there, just as here, is real, life-changing discipleship.

What would I say to any pastor or church leader who may be beginning the process of shifting his church to a discipleship model? Keep your heart warm and your vision clear. Everything in this world is passing away, so set your affection on things above. Get your eye on the glory of God. Look to the day when the nations have finally heard the gospel, and the redeemed of the Lord are gathered around the throne to praise the Lamb forever. This is eternal reality. Anything that does not contribute to this destiny is an exercise in futility.

DISCIPLESHIFT AND YOUR CHURCH

As you close this book, I realize that we've worked through a lot of areas together. This amount of information takes a while to process, and I encourage you and your team to move slowly, carefully, and wisely.

If I could leave you with one thought, it would be this: God's church works.

Say those words out loud if you need to. They're beautiful words, and they're absolutely true. When I say, "God's church works," I do not mean that it is pain free or that it works perfectly. What I mean is that people will be saved and discipled, in spite of the fact that we are in a war and at times will lose a battle and even get wounded. However, God has called you to your church for such a time as this. The encouragement is that if we'll be in relationship with God, his Word, and others, then he will step in and bring people to himself through his church, which you're privileged to lead. God will grow this people up to spiritual maturity. Philippians 1:6 says, "I am sure of this, that he who began a good work in you will bring it to completion at the day of Jesus Christ" (ESV).

Keep in mind that your goal as a church leader is to have an authentic relationship with God, and then to do things as a team through the body of Christ. The results of that will reflect the blessing of God in big ways.

KEY POINTS

- This book purposely doesn't tell you all the specifics of the steps you need to take to begin to implement discipleship in your church. It's more strategic that way. It's best for your church if you and your leadership team take the principles in this book and wrestle with them as they relate to your unique practices, traditions, and corporate structures, as well as the context you live in.
- The goal as church leaders isn't to accumulate a crowd and impart information to them. It's not to create an emotional experience that will keep people charged up for a few hours or days and make them

want to come back so they can feel it again. The shift is that we need to raise up biblical disciples and deploy them into the world so they can raise up other disciples. These disciples are to grow into accurate copies of Jesus who rightly deliver his message in his ways.

- As you begin to implement discipleship, the large-scale steps are fivefold: (1) as a team, develop the biblical vision for your church; (2) as a team, create a common language and definition of terms; (3) as a team, develop the process for creating disciples, then put this process into the hands of the frontline soldiers; (4) consistently live out your vision, and consistently recast your vision; (5) constantly assess, correct course, and encourage.

ACKNOWLEDGMENTS

This book is dedicated to the elders of Real Life Ministries and Harpeth Community Church. We dedicate it in gratitude and appreciation for these leaders, who have taken the DiscipleShift journey with us.

Many thanks to the cofounders of the Relational Discipleship Network, Luke Yetter and Jerry Harris. We also thank our friends Todd Wilson and Exponential Network, Ryan Pazdur and all the team at Zondervan, Greg Johnson and the WordServe Literary Group, and especially editor Marcus Brotherton.

NOTES

1. According to the research reported in chapter 1 of *Transformational Discipleship: How People Really Grow* (Nashville: B&H, 2012), by Eric Geiger, Michael Kelley, and Philip Nation, there is a disconnection in many churches between church leaders' perceptions about the effectiveness of discipleship in their churches and objective evidence of true discipleship and transformation. Pastors tend to focus on anecdotal evidence (individuals who talk about how the church has helped them) instead of on factual evidence.

2. The most comprehensive summary and discussion of this research is still Ronald Sider's book *The Scandal of the Evangelical Conscience: Why Are Christians Living Just Like the Rest of the World?* (Grand Rapids, Mich.: Baker, 2005). George Barna looks at the broader context of these things in his many books, including his recent book *Futurecast: What Today's Trends Mean for Tomorrow's World* (BarnaBooks, 2011). And David Olson describes the true state of church involvement in his book *The American Church in Crisis* (Grand Rapids, Mich.: Zondervan, 2008). See lots of research and updates in George Barna and David Kinnaman's extensive research on these and related matters at *barna.org*.

3. David Kinnaman, *You Lost Me: Why Young Christians Are Leaving Church ... and Rethinking Faith* (Grand Rapids, Mich.: Baker, 2011) and David Kinnaman and Gabe Lyons, *UnChristian: What a New Generation Really Thinks about Christianity ... and Why It Matters* (Grand Rapids, Mich.; Baker, 2007).

4. Matt Branaugh, "Willow Creek's Huge Shift: Influential Megachurch Moves Away from Seeker-Sensitive Services." Posted May 15, 2008. *Christianity Today: christianitytoday.com/ct/2008/june/5.13.html* (accessed March 2012).

5. Bill Hybels, foreword to Greg Hawkins and Cally Parkinson, *Reveal: Where Are You?* (Barrington, Ill.: Willow Creek Resources, 2007), 3.

6. UrL Scaramanga, "Willow Creek Repents? Why the Most Influential Church in America Now Says 'We Made a Mistake.'" Posted October 18, 2007. *Out of Ur: outofur.com/archives/2007/10/willow_creek_re.html* (accessed May 11, 2012).

7. In 2010, the number was 85 percent. See George Barna, *Futurecast* (Carol Stream, Ill.: Tyndale, 2011), Kindle location 124.

8. Kevin DeYoung and Greg Gilbert, *What Is the Mission of the Church? Making Sense of Social Justice, Shalom, and the Great Commission* (Wheaton, Ill.: Good News/Crossway, 2011), Kindle location 265.

9. Michael Wilkins, *Following the Master: A Biblical Theology of Discipleship* (Grand Rapids, Mich.: Zondervan, 1992), 42.

10. Dallas Willard, *The Great Omission: Reclaiming Jesus' Essential Teachings on Discipleship* (New York: HarperOne, 2006), xi.

11. The participles in vv. 19–20 are subordinate to "make disciples" and explain how disciples are made: by "baptizing" them and "teaching" them obedience to all of Jesus' commandments. The first of these involves the decisive initiation into discipleship, and the second proves a perennially incomplete, lifelong task. See Craig Bloomberg, *Matthew: An Exegetical and Theological Exposition of Holy Scripture*, The New American Commentary (Nashville: Broadman, 1992), 431.

12. To learn more about relational discipleship with our children, see *Dedicated!* by Bobby Harrington, Jason Houser, and Chad Harrington (forthcoming).

13. In what follows, we utilize Kevin Vanhoozer's language for understanding truth more holistically, as it impacts us intellectually, emotionally, and volitionally. See *Whatever Happened to Truth?* by Andreas Köstenberger, R. Albert Mohler Jr., J. P. Moreland, and Keven J. Vanhoozer (Wheaton, Ill.: Crossway, 2005), 123. Biblical scholar and early church history expert Everett Ferguson also advocates a definition of faith that is holistic in this same way, as "it involves the intellect, the emotion, and the will." See *The Church of Christ: A Biblical Ecclesiology for Today* (Grand Rapids, Mich.: Eerdmans, 1997), 165–69.

14. Spiritual formation is a big topic, and we are grateful for writers such as Richard Foster, Dallas Willard, John Ortberg, and others who describe how the Holy Spirit brings change. In this book, we focus more on the relational components used by the Holy Spirit to develop Christlike people. If we had more space, we would use it to advocate spiritual practices and disciplines. We are grateful for those who teach us about these habits and commend them to our readers.

15. To work through the following material at an in-depth level, see Avery T. Willis Jr., Jim Putman, Bill Krause, and Brandon Guindon, *Real-Life Discipleship Training Manual: Equipping Disciples Who Make Disciples* (Colorado Springs: NavPress, 2010). To read a nonworkbook summary, see Jim Putman, *Real-Life Discipleship: Building Churches That Make Disciples* (Colorado Springs: NavPress, 2010).

16. To learn more about the Relational Discipleship Network and the Disciple-Shift Experiential Training, go to *relationaldiscipleshipnetwork.com*.

17. The findings featured in *Move* suggest, in general, that spiritual growth progresses across a continuum of four segments, moving from those who are Exploring Christ to those who are Christ-Centered. Unfortunately, becoming a spiritual parent or discipler is not clearly articulated in the general presentation in their continuum. See Greg Hawkins and Cally Parkinson, *Move: What 1,000 Churches Reveal about Spiritual Growth* (Grand Rapids, Mich.: Zondervan, 2011), Kindle locations 344–45.

18. Geiger, Kelley, and Nation, *Transformational Discipleship*, Kindle locations 1431–37.

19. See also 1 Corinthians 3:1; 14:19–21; and Ephesians 4:14–15.

20. See also John 13:33; 1 Corinthians 4:14; 14:20; and Galatians 4:19, where Jesus and Paul refer to believers as children.

21. See also 1 Corinthians 13:11; 14:20; Colossians 4:12; Philippians 3:15; and James 1:4.

22. See also 1 Corinthians 4:14; 2 Corinthians 6:13; 12:14–15; Galatians 4:19; Philippians 2:22; 1 Thessalonians 2:7–8, 11; and 3 John 1:4.

23. Mike Breen and Alex Absalom provide more background on these spaces and church life. See *Launching Missional Communities* (Pawleys Island, S.C.: 3DM, 2010), Kindle locations 943–49.

24. Another book we recommend is M. Scott Boren's *The Relational Way* (Houston: Touch, 2007).

25. For spiritual seekers, large church services can be very beneficial if they (1) help people in developing a personal relationship with Christ, (2) provide compelling worship services, and (3) provide a feeling of belonging. See Hawkins and Parkinson, *Move*, Kindle locations 429–30.

26. Bill Hull has some good information on this point in his book *The Disciple-Making Pastor: Leading Others on the Journey of Faith*, rev. ed. (Grand Rapids, Mich.: Baker, 2007). "The confusion over the words shepherd and pastor has motivated me to seek a modern equivalent, a word widely understood by contemporary society that fits the job description of Ephesians 4. That word is coach" (Kindle locations 1112–13).

27. We have heard this number used by various church leaders, and it matches the observations we have made in many churches.

28. Willow Creek's *Reveal* studies show that in the average church, stalled or dissatisfied people account for one out of four church congregants. See Hawkins and Parkinson, *Move*, Kindle locations 238–39.

29. See Markus Barth, *Ephesians: Introduction, Translation, and Commentary on*

Chapters 1–3, Anchor Bible, vol. 34 (Garden City, N.Y.: Doubleday, 1960), 32–36, and Alan Hirsch, *The Forgotten Ways: Reactivating the Missional Church* (Grand Rapids: Brazos, 2007), 151 and *http://www.theforgottenways .org/apest/* (accessed January 15, 2011).

30. Dave Ferguson and Jon Ferguson, *Exponential: How You and Your Friends Can Start a Missional Church Movement* (Grand Rapids, Mich.: Zondervan, 2010), 63.

31. Almost every in-depth analysis of the state of discipleship in the church today points to the supreme need for people to get into the Word of God and apply it to their lives. See Geiger, Kelley, and Nation, *Transformational Discipleship*, Kindle locations 910–18. Bill Hybels summarizes the results of the massive *Reveal* studies: "We learned that the most effective strategy for moving people forward in their journey of faith is biblical engagement. Not just getting people into the Bible when they're in church—which we do quite well—but helping them engage the Bible on their own outside of church" (Hawkins and Parkinson, *Move*, Kindle locations 71–72).

32. Rebecca Barnes and Lindy Lowry, "7 Startling Facts: An Up Close Look at Church Attendance in America." *ChurchLeaders: churchleaders.com/pastors/ pastor-articles/139575–7-startling-facts-an-up-close-look-at-church-attendance- in-america.html* (accessed August 11, 2012).

33. This story and much of this information is recounted by Bobby Harrington in the book *Church Planting from the Ground Up*, ed. Tom Jones (Joplin, Mo.: College Press, 2004), 238–49.

34. "The Engel Scale Explained," *http://www.internetevangelismday.com/engel- scale.php* (accessed November 17, 2012). For the whole perspective in book form, see James F. Engel and Wilbert H. Norton, *What's Gone Wrong with the Harvest?* (Grand Rapids, Mich.: Zondervan, 1975).

35. Thom Rainer and Eric Geiger offer some practical help in this regard in their book *Simple Church* (Nashville: Broadman, 2006), 165–95.

36. Jim Putman, *Real-Life Discipleship: Building Churches That Make Disciples* (Colorado Springs: NavPress, 2010), 55–64.

37. Hull, *Disciple-Making Pastor*. "I contend that measuring a church by bod- ies, bucks, and buildings means nothing more than having 'the right fluff'" (Kindle locations 1696–97).

38. Reggie McNeal makes some suggestions about new scorecards that will con- nect with many, but we believe that the fruits of relational discipleship should be the basis of a scorecard. See Reggie McNeal, *Missional Renaissance: Chang- ing the Scorecard for the CHURCH* (San Francisco: Jossey-Bass, 2009). See in particular pages 111–27.

39. Note briefly the doctrine of the priesthood of all believers. First Peter 2:4–10 clearly sets out the foundation. The book of Hebrews shows how Jesus takes away the sins of all believers (Heb. 9:28), makes all believers perfect (10:14), and invites every believer to enter the Most Holy Place by the blood of Jesus (10:19) as priests in Christ. We're all called "children of God" in Galatians 3:26. All believers are given spiritual gifts, according to 1 Corinthians 12 (and other passages), and "each one of you is a part" of the body of Christ (1 Cor. 12:27). Every pastor's job is to equip the saints (Eph. 4:11–13) and to present them mature in Christ Jesus (Col. 1:28).

40. For more information, go to *relationaldiscipleshipnetwork.com*.

41. See Sam Rainer, "Ten Questions for Formulating a Discipleship Process." Published January 18, 2009. *Church Forward: http://samrainer.wordpress .com/2009/01/18/ten-questions-for-formulating-a-discipleship-process/* (accessed March 25, 2010).

ABOUT THE AUTHORS

Jim Putman is the founder and senior pastor of Real Life Ministries in Post Falls, Idaho. Real Life Ministries began as a small group in 1998 and has grown to a membership of more than eight thousand. Real Life was launched with a commitment to discipleship and the model of discipleship Jesus practiced, which is called "relational discipleship." Ninety percent of the people are active in small groups. *Outreach* magazine continually lists Real Life Ministries among the top one hundred most influential churches in America. Jim is the founding leader of the new Relational Discipleship Network. Jim holds degrees from Boise State University and Boise Bible College. His voice reaches hundreds of thousands across the nation through speaking conferences, the web, radio, and weekend services. He is the author of three books: *Church Is a Team Sport, Real-Life Discipleship*, and *Real-Life Discipleship Workbook* (with Avery Willis and others). Jim's passion is discipleship through small groups. With his background in sports and coaching, he believes in the value of strong coaching as a means to disciple others. He lives with his wife and three sons in scenic northern Idaho.

Dr. Bobby Harrington is the founding and lead pastor of Harpeth Community Church, just beside the Harpeth River, south of Nashville, in Franklin, Tennessee. Harpeth Community Church was launched in 1998 as an "attractional church" that is now making the transition to being a "relational discipleship church." Bobby holds four theological degrees including the master of divinity degree from Harding Graduate School of Religion and the doctor of ministry degree from Southern Baptist Theological Seminary. Along with Jim Putman, Bobby is one of the founders of the new Relational

Discipleship Network. Bobby served as the director of research, development, and missional leadership for Stadia, a national church-planting organization. He was Stadia's lead trainer of church planters, and as such, he trained hundreds of church planters from 2003 through 2011. He helped pioneer their national church-planting network system. He was also the president of Church Coaching Solutions from 2005 through 2010. He is the author of *Together: Networks and Church Planting* (with Marcus Bigelow) and *To Trust and Follow Jesus: Relational Discipleship as the Core Mission of the Church*. Bobby is married to Cindy, with two children, Ashley and Chad. Bobby and Chad are joining Jason Houser (of Seeds Family Worship) to publish a book on relational discipleship for parents called *Dedicate!*

Dr. Robert E. Coleman is a legend in the evangelical community. At eighty-four, he continues to serve as a professor at various seminaries, including his role as Distinguished Senior Professor of Discipleship and Evangelism at Gordon-Conwell Theological Seminary. Dr. Coleman is a prolific author, having written hundreds of articles and twenty-one books, including *The Master Plan of Evangelism*, which has sold multiple million copies and is the book for which he is best known. He directed the School of World Mission and Evangelism at Trinity Evangelical Divinity School for eighteen years, and prior to that, taught for many years at Asbury Theological Seminary. From 1989 – 2001 he led the Institute of Evangelism in the Billy Graham Center at Wheaton College and served as dean of the Billy Graham International Schools of Evangelism. He is also a founding member of the Lausanne Committee for World Evangelism and a past president of the Academy for Evangelism in Theological Education. His personal interests center on spending time with his family, all his children and grandchildren, and keeping in touch with people he has discipled.

ABOUT THE EXPONENTIAL SERIES

The interest in church planting has grown significantly in recent years. The need for new churches has never been greater. At the same time, the number of models and approaches is expanding. To address the unique opportunities of churches in this landscape, Exponential Network, in partnership with Leadership Network and Zondervan, launched the Exponential Series in 2010.

Books in this series:

- Tell the reproducing church story.
- Celebrate the diversity of models and approaches God is using to reproduce healthy congregations.
- Highlight the innovative and pioneering practices of healthy reproducing churches.
- Equip, inspire, and challenge kingdom-minded leaders with the tools they need in their journey of becoming reproducing church leaders.

Exponential exists to attract, inspire, and equip kingdom-minded leaders to engage in a movement of high-impact, reproducing churches. We provide a national voice for this movement through the Exponential Conference, the Exponential Initiative, Exponential Venture, and the Exponential Series.

Leadership Network exists to accelerate the impact of 100X leaders. Believing that meaningful conversations and strategic connections can change the world, we seek to help leaders navigate the future by exploring new ideas and finding application for each unique context.

For more information about the Exponential Series, go to *http://www.exponential.org/exponentialseries.*

9 780310 492627